School Leadership

CH00960161

'Pat Thomson outlines in graphic and sometimes sho~~cking detail the complexities~~ of school headship ... [and outlines] the risks, stresses and dissatisfactions of real leadership in real schools.'
Stephen J Ball, *Karl Mannheim Professor of Sociology of Education, University of London*

Most teachers become heads for idealistic reasons, wanting to make a difference to the lives of children and young people. Yet serving heads suggest the job is getting harder, talking openly about stress and leaving the job. Many teachers now see headship as a risky business, and succession planning, while necessary, will not on its own be sufficient to attract the diverse range of applicants required to satisfactorily fill leadership positions. *School Leadership: Heads on the Block?* addresses this shortage. It suggests there is no crisis in supply *per se*, but that schools in some locations find it difficult to attract the 'right people with the right stuff'. The book examines the expectations of heads, the hours they are expected to work and the nature of everyday demands. It proposes that 'sudden death' accountabilities act as a major disincentive to potential applicants, and outlines a series of policy measures to tackle the kinds of daily pressures heads now experience.

Key features of the book:

- draws on a wide range of material, ranging from published research, interviews and media clippings, to popular films and children's novels;
- makes extensive use of headteachers' words and stories;
- based on the author's own experiences of headship, tackling issues that leadership books often ignore.

The book will be of interest to headteachers, headteachers' professional associations, teachers and those who study teaching. It will be useful to policymakers, those responsible for the education of potential heads and for headteacher professional development.

Pat Thomson is Professor of Education and Director of Research at the School of Education, University of Nottingham, UK. She has worked as a headteacher in disadvantaged schools in South Australia, and has published several books, including *Helping Doctoral Students Write* and *Doing Visual Research with Children and Young People*.

School Leadership

Heads on the Block?

Pat Thomson

 Routledge
Taylor & Francis Group

LONDON AND NEW YORK

First published 2009 by Routledge
2 Park Square, Milton Park, Abingdon, Oxon, OX14 4RN

Simultaneously published in the USA and Canada
by Routledge
29 West 35th Street, New York, NY 10001
Routledge is an imprint of the Taylor & Francis Group, an informa business

© 2009 Pat Thomson

Typeset in Garamond and Scala Sans by Taylor & Francis Books
Printed and bound in Great Britain by
TJ International, Padstow, Cornwall

British Library Cataloguing in Publication Data
A catalogue record for this book is available from the British Library

Library of Congress Cataloging in Publication Data
Thomson, Pat, 1948-
School leadership : heads on the block / Pat Thomson.
p. cm.
Includes bibliographical references.
1. School principals – England. 2. School principals – Australia. I. Title.
LB2831.926.G7T47 2009
371.2'012 – dc22
2008033869

ISBN10: 0-415-43073-9 (hbk)
ISBN 10: 0-415-43075-5 (pbk)

ISBN13: 978-0-415-43073-9 (hbk)
ISBN 13: 978-0-415-43075-3 (pbk)

For 'Dave' and 'Sandra'

Contents

List of boxes

Acknowledgements

A book such as this is not a solo effort and there are many people to thank. First of all, the necessarily anonymous headteachers in Australia and England who willingly gave of their time to tell their stories. Many of these narratives were funny, optimistic and inspirational but some were shocking, painful, and sad. I have endeavoured to deal with these working lives in ways that are ethical and just and I hope that this is evident. Second, there are my research colleagues who allowed me to re-read some data from related projects in order to check understandings and verify claims. Their intellectual work and writings have informed the ways in which this book has developed.

A little of this work has appeared before. The story of Ian George first appeared in P. Thomson (2003) 'No more Managers-R-Us! Researching/ teaching about head teachers and "schools in challenging circumstances"', *Journal of Education Policy* 18(3): 333–45. Some of the media examples in Chapter 5 appeared in P. Thomson, J. Blackmore, J. Sachs and K. Tregenza (2003) 'High stakes principalship: sleepless nights, heart attacks and sudden death accountabilities. Reading media representations of the US principal shortage', *Australian Journal of Education* 47(2): 118–32. The extract on pp. 138 is taken from R.B. Briner, S. Poppleton, S. Owens and T. Keifer (2008) *The Nature, Causes and Consequences of Harm in Emotionally-Demanding Occupations* (Norwich: Health and Safety Executive) and used with permission.

I most particularly need to acknowledge the importance of ongoing conversations and projects with my academic soulmates Jill Blackmore and Helen Gunter – not to mention the retail therapy. My current Nottingham colleagues, in particular Christopher Day and Christine Hall, helped me to come to terms with living and working in England and I don't tell them often enough how important they have been to me. The work of some of my doctoral students – John Churchley, Sally Coulton, Bob Curtis and Daphne Whiteoak – both stimulated and moderated the arguments here. I would also like to thank Mick Brookes from the National Association of Head Teachers (NAHT) for his encouragement. Jill Blackmore, Peter Gronn, Helen Gunter and Belinda Harris read this text in its penultimate form and provided more additional references than I could use, invaluable reassurance and feedback about inaccuracies. Needless to say, any that remain are entirely my responsibility.

I had practical assistance in the writing of this book. The School of Education granted me some study leave and Melanie Walker, Peter Gates, Monica Mclean and the team in the research office picked up the administrative flotsam I left behind. Phillip Mudd, Alistair Shaw and the team at Routledge provided ongoing support: I do promise that one day I will write a book without having to extend the deadline. My partner Randy Barber not only lived through two decades of school administration and another in the university, but also the production of this book. It is undoubtedly true that I couldn't have done any of it without him. Finally, a note to Simon: this is still not the book about what it's like when your Mum is a headteacher. I haven't forgotten and I'll get round to that soon – but of course you've heard that before.

Introduction

Headship is risky business

There have been a lot of books written about school leadership in the past few years. The vast majority of them talk about what good or effective or successful leaders do. The message of these books is that 'this is how you do it'. There are a few books that are written by headteachers themselves or which feature lengthy interviews with heads; in these we read a personal story of trials, tribulations and triumphs in a particular school. Such narratives can end up being heroic tales of 'I did it my way', but in most personal accounts readers can almost smell, taste, and hear the everyday life of schools. There are also books which aspire to 'tell it like it is'. These books are based on research. Two of the best known are Harry Wolcott's (1973) pioneering *The Man in the Principal's Office* and Geoff Southworth's (1995) *Looking into Primary Headship*, both of which use extensive observation of a single head-teacher at work. These research-based books share with the first group an ambition to have an impact on policy and practice, and with the second, a desire to present a narrative that 'rings true' to serving school leaders.

This book falls into the third category. Its focus is unashamedly on head-teachers and their everyday work. This does not signal advocacy of a model of heroic leadership or a return to 'great man' theories of leadership. It is certainly true that headteachers are not the only ones in a school who exercise leader-ship and that schools simply could not work if that was the case. But the way that leadership is shared is dependent on the head: through their use of symbolic systems and management structures, she/he can do things to make the school more, or less, democratic and more or less inclusive of others. And there *is* something very particular about the leadership/management expected of and practised by those in the 'top job'. It *is* different in important ways from work undertaken by others in the senior management team, governors, heads of department and team leaders. This book focuses on these particula-rities and argues that the headteacher's leadership/management is more than simply a way of doing things, it is also a way of being in and knowing about the world. It is a job with very particular benefits – and very particular costs.

The book is based on my own experience of headship. It is in some senses autobiographical, in that it seeks to bring to the fore aspects of headship that

I know to be important. But the book is also based on research into the work of English and Australian headteachers, and draws on a corpus of interview data and text analysis accumulated over a decade. It is also inevitably idiosyncratic, in that it sometimes draws on an ongoing fascination with the way that education appears in news media and popular fiction, films and television. This latter interest is perhaps symptomatic of a former English (the school subject) teacher, but equally arises from the myriad of conversations I had as a headteacher with young people about what they were reading and watching and what it all meant.

The purpose of the book is to highlight some of the contemporary pressures, dilemmas and tensions that surround the headship. It is intended for readers interested in what is happening to relatively significant numbers of headteachers. Some will want to argue that not all heads are like these in this book, and of course this is true. There are very many heads who are happy, healthy and highly successful. I suggest that chance plays a part in these best-case scenarios: most heads are acutely aware that their good fortune is not all of their own making. Other researchers (e.g. Day, 2003; Leithwood and Day, 2007; Leithwood *et al.*, 2006) are currently writing about this 'successful' group, and their work should be read in conjunction with this less rosy picture. This book *is* a deliberately selective view – as is all research. I am particularly concerned with those heads who are not always happy with their lot; this interest is not simply for its own sake, although that too would be acceptable. Here I am concerned with how particular aspects of headteachers' work relate to questions of 'supply' (the diminishing number of applicants for headteacher posts) and 'retention' (the number of serving heads who leave their post prematurely).

Since a goal of the book is to try to understand circumstances and events from the points of view of those who experience them, both interview and some published textual data were subject to interpretive narrative analysis; that is, I looked for 'embedded stories' (Clandinin and Connelly, 2000; Josselson and Lieblich, 1995; Lieblich *et al.*, 1998; Riessman, 1993). These were then edited in order to produce 'voiced' narratives which retain something of the speech patterns and lexicon of the interviewees (Britzman, 1994). I then selected from the larger corpus some 'not a-typical' stories. These are presented in text boxes (although Chapter 7 presents longer narratives within three 'story' sections) to signify that these are *representations* of the interviewee's 'voices' (cf. Smyth and Hattam, 2001). Clearly, these are not 'authentic' (Winter, 2002), although I hope they do 'ring true' (Garman, 1994), particularly to headteachers themselves. One chapter (Chapter 3) relies on a detailed 'content analysis' (Silverman, 1993) of texts and I make use throughout the book of media articles which have been, like interview data, subject to narrative analysis. I also make extensive use of published research. Wherever possible, I have used research that heads themselves have conducted and/or commissioned. A comprehensive literature review underpins what is cited: I conducted a 'mapping of the field' (Kamler and Thomson, 2006) rather than the more contentious 'evidence-based' approach. I have given some details of numbers and methods used in the statistical studies, and interested readers can pursue these studies further in order to critically assess their methodological 'blank and blind spots' (Wagner, 1993).

Throughout the book, and in this chapter, I use the term 'headteacher' rather than 'principal'. I am persuaded by the British argument that retention of the word teaching in the job title is significant, just as was the removal of the words 'master' and 'mistress' which implied that the job was somehow tied to particular gendered qualities and characteristics. While the term 'principal' is used in most parts of the world, and is increasingly used in England, the notion of being a teacher is important to the argument made in the text.

The book develops a conception of the headship as 'risky business'. This is an argument that I began to make as I was leaving the headship. In 1997, I produced a discussion paper for the South Australian Principals Association which focused on the uncertainties faced by school leaders/managers at a time when school systems were increasingly calling for certainty via linear strategic plans and numerical goals (Thomson, 1997). A little later I decided that the notion of 'risk' (Beck, 1992) was an apt term for the reality and the 'feeling' of contemporary headship. At the time, I wrote that

> [being a head was] now a risky business. As a group and as individuals we are increasingly placed in situations where we have to make difficult choices, where we have to manage multiple agendas and communities and where there are often no easy, right or quick solutions. Living and working in, and with, such uncertainty forces us to rely more and more on our own individual and collective resources.
>
> (Thomson, 1999)

I explain this approach in this chapter. The remainder of the book considers headship as risky business, the shortage of applicants for the headship as a risky policy agenda and the actions of potential applicants and serving heads as one of risk calculation and in some cases, risk avoidance and/or harm minimization. I spend some time elaborating the nature of those risks, some of which are unavoidable, some of which are unpredictable, and some of which are manufactured and therefore amenable to change.

Working in an insecure and uncertain world

Social commentators argue that one of the key characteristics of the times is the proliferation of risks and risk-consciousness. In his book, *Risk Society* (1992), Ulrich Beck proposes that we now live in a time of 'manufactured risk'. He notes that the historical project of unstoppable progress and growth – made possible by the application of the sciences, rational ways of thinking and technological advances to all areas of the physical life world – has now produced a world in which nothing is untouched by human existence. He proposes that, rather than bringing us peace and security, we have via this mode of progress *made* risks for ourselves that now threaten not only our way of life, but also ultimately our very lives. Beck reasons that these kinds of global risks cannot be left alone. They must be attended to. However, the very act of addressing them brings a new set of risks. We are, he suggests, now trapped in a permanent state of identifying, addressing and manufacturing risks.

A corollary of the risk society is that everyone has to think about their actions, since they can no longer rely on experts to make decisions for them. The divergence of increasingly specialized and warring experts, and ready access to information via the new technologies, requires lay people to exercise considerably more discrimination than they have in previous times. Almost *all* decisions entail weighing up diverse and contradictory information, rather than just relying on tradition, or the way 'things have always been done around here' (Beck *et al.*, 1994; Giddens, 1990, 1991). Beck argues that the growth of risk society has made three practices integral to everyday life:

1 *risk assessment* – the development of calculative practices which anticipate possible risks;
2 *risk avoidance* – taking decisions based on the potential for adverse consequences;
3 *risk management planning* – the development of rational plans to be used when risks become reality to deal with effects and prevent them spreading.

Clearly not everyone is equally positioned in relation to risk and to choice. Some people have far fewer choices than others by virtue of who they are, their social, economic and political circumstances, and their individual and collective histories. Nor are risks distributed equally. The consequences of apparently similar decisions can be very different depending on context and circumstances. Those who are poor, for example, often have less choice and face greater risks than those who are more comfortable (Bauman, 1998). A young person's decision to leave school without qualifications often plays out very differently for those whose families have significantly greater educational cultural and financial assets and networks, than for those who live in isolated ex-manufacturing neighbourhoods where there is little work.

The three risk practices, in the context of the decline of traditional sources of authority, the questioning of expertise and the rise of a general DIY self-help orientation to problems, are now embedded in our everyday life. One arena where this happens is in relation to work and careers.

The changing nature of work

It is now widely recognized that both the nature of work and the shape of careers are changing. We are said to be entering a globalized 'knowledge economy' where there are fewer well-paid positions for those who do not have comparatively good levels of education. In Western countries, the 1980s saw the development of sophisticated industrial technologies which reduced the number of unskilled jobs. At the same time, significant numbers of transnational companies began to change locations to find cheaper resources and labour. Entire workforces found themselves suddenly left behind with little ready or steady employment (Casey, 1995; Reich, 1991). Today, in addition to 'knowledge work', there is a burgeoning and often very badly paid services sector (Eirenreich, 2001; Toynbee, 2003), a proliferation of relatively pedestrian data-related jobs, and work in a range of shadow and black[1] economies (Kenway *et al.*, 2006).

The conventions of economic and organization theory, management and government policy have shifted in concert with these changed global conditions. Companies now talk of themselves as less hierarchical and networked, with much of what formerly happened in-house now 'outsourced' to chains of preferred suppliers. So that they can move quickly to cope with rapidly changing economic circumstances, many organizations have shifted to 'core' and 'casual' workforces so that staff costs can be cut and new staff hired in tune with the company bottom-line (Handy, 1994; Peters, 1992). At the same time, many governments have embraced more free market policies. Rather than stimulate the economy by undertaking large amounts of public works and public services as they did in post-war boom years, nation-states have contractualized and privatized much of what they do, also introducing internal market mechanisms such as tendering, contracts and targets in order to get 'value for money' (Bauman, 2002; Harvey, 2005). One of the consequences of the shifts in organizational and governance practice is that it is not only those traditionally involved in blue-collar work whose jobs are now less certain. Middle management is also affected, and the consequences of an abrupt redundancy play out for many in fractured family life and a more fragile state of emotional/mental health (Eirenreich, 2005; Sennett, 1998).

Most people in and out of employment now find themselves with what is called a 'portfolio career' (Handy, 1995) where, rather than having a job for life, people now have serial jobs and even serial professions. In these changed work and career arrangements, the onus for retraining is often placed on the individual. However, while some seek that old-fashioned sense of certainty and security, many employees happily become transient, and their managers have to work hard to win and keep their loyalty and services. Working life has become for many a 'choice biography' (see Dwyer and Wynn, 2001), a process of managing an ongoing set of decisions, rather than following a predetermined pathway. For some, there might be an overall strategic goal against which current decisions can be assessed. For others, forging a career is a more pragmatic process of what seems to be the best or the least damaging option at the time. And one factor in work decision-making is how risky the job appears to be to security, health and relationships.

These changes in work and career have implications for and manifestations in education, not only because schools are where future workers are educated, but also for the profession itself (Hargreaves, 2003). In line with changes in work and career more generally, many young people now beginning teaching do not see it as a life-long career, but as one of a number of things they might do. Teaching has become a portable qualification which travels between countries but also between occupations and industries. The shift to knowledge-based work now means that industry and government are interested in learning and they seek those with educational qualifications. At the same time, education systems themselves are morphing into new forms. There are new mixes of professional and para-professional jobs within schools. Schools and colleges are no longer permanent fixtures of local neighbourhoods and are frequently restructured, amalgamated, closed and re-opened. Leadership structures too are becoming more varied, with new forms of networked and federated organization now in operation. A career in education is thus less fixed/more uncertain than it used to be.

This means that teachers, just like other workers, are now *much* more likely to engage in the evaluative choice processes of risk assessment and risk avoidance in order to decide what work avenues to pursue.

The changing nature of leadership and management

The 'risk society' also has implications for leaders/managers. Organizations now seek to minimize risk at all costs (Hutter and Power, 2005). This pursuit of safety is a relatively recent phenomenon and is not carried out to the same degree or the same way in all parts of the world. Some societies, for example, regard risk-taking as a normal part of growing up, and are mystified by decisions to avoid an activity on the grounds that it might be dangerous. Rather, such pastimes are undertaken with due care. However, in many parts of the world, the search for safety and security has become a 'moral imperative' for individuals and institutions (McWilliam and Singh, 2004). They now have to have 'the right stuff' to reduce the possibility of harm (Douglas, 1992). To be and to do good is equated with the identification of events, activities and occasions which might prove risky, while 'being bad' applies to individuals who might place themselves and others 'at risk' (Lupton, 1999).

'The risk management of everything' now appears to be *the* logical way of doing things (Power, 2004). All responsible administrators shoulder risk management obligations. Because what counts as risk and its management is just as debatable as any other matter, institutions lay down what appear as a plethora of administrative rules and standards (Hood *et al.*, 2001), but these are equally moral requirements. Leaders and managers are expected to assess actual and potential hazards and occurrences and to attend to them if they exist. If they have not yet happened, they must have a plan about what to do, if they do. This prudential process can be very time-consuming and it often appears to have little pay-off other than the production of hefty documents available for inspection. Yet these are perceived as vital in staving off damage to 'reputational risk', because no organization or individual administrator can afford to be caught apparently unprepared (Power, 2007).

The consequences for not having adequate risk management in place can be severe. Yet planning to manage risks is no guarantee of safety, and is sometimes the reverse. Studies of major disasters suggest that a focus on calculating probabilities often creates a false sense of security and safety which can result in insufficient attention to the possible causes of a disaster. The classic case is the *Exxon Valdez* oil spill. Budget cuts to maintenance and replacement schedules were not factored into copious risk management plans and this, combined with the use of detergent to deal with oil spills, a solution which was tested in a laboratory rather than in the actual weather conditions which prevail in most ship-wrecks, contributed to an environmental catastrophe. Risk management and disaster plans also often assume levels of coordination, communication and rationality which are not achievable, and pose solutions which are untested and which fail in reality. In other words, the practices of risk management often produce as much risk as they do its avoidance and management (Clarke, 1999).

Politicians and policy-makers in particular are now wedded to the quest for security and the appearance of certainty. Political parties do not get elected if they cannot promise sure-fire and short-term fixes for all social woes. They are vulnerable to charges that they have acted in contradictory ways, or have changed their mind. Their very legitimacy is created through acting in ways that appear to enhance safety and security and decrease and manage risk. In the political game, being *seen* to be in control is as important as the reality. Even with things that are out of the reach of government – the value of currency, decisions to move sites of production – the government must seem to manage them.

The quest for certainty and for the simulation of control via risk leadership/management plays out in education. Across the Western world we can see a proliferation of, and an increased assuredness of, strategic plans – *All* children will ... Schools *must ensure* ... Principals *will provide* ... – accompanied by the production of statistical data, indicators, targets and benchmarks that purportedly represent the reality of school life. These plans and auditing documents become the daily stuff of headteachers' in-trays. Headteachers must deal with these plans even if they suspect that they are undeliverable and/or hopelessly idealistic and unrealistic (Perry, 2006; Perry and McWilliam, 2007). They find themselves presenting their schools and themselves – upwards to policy-makers, outwards to parents and the community, and inwards to staff and students – as sure about things they hold to be important and confident in government policy. No matter how risky actual circumstances and plans are, and no matter how uncertain leaders/managers feel on the inside, they must *appear* to be in control.

But if there is one thing that educators know it is that learning is often associated with risks. The assimilation of existing knowledge is integral to learning, but an overemphasis on regurgitation of prescribed material leads to a failure to experiment, to dream of possibilities, to explore potential avenues and to face the reality of making a mistake (Craft *et al.*, 2001; Loveless, 2002). Such productive risky learning is not simply good for children but also for adults, and not simply good for individuals but also organizations (Bilton, 2007; Henry, 2006). In this light, Beck's concerns about prevention of risk take on another dimension, for it is possible that in seeking to prevent risk, the manufactured consequence is that there is reduced opportunity for learning or improvement.

The dilemmas around control, risk, and safety and the pressure of proof – and the consequences for headteachers and for prospective headteachers of having to work with and around systems of risk management – are integral to this book. Its prime focus is on:

1 the ways in which those thinking about applying for, or staying in, the headship assess it and experience it as a job where the risks are worth taking;
2 what risk management planning is, and might be, put in place to minimize the potential damage which arises when educational systems do not have enough people to lead and manage schools.

The 'supply problem' is explored in Part I.

Part I

Understanding the supply problem

Part I introduces the problem of headteacher supply. It argues that lack of applications for headship, combined with the numbers of heads who leave prior to retirement, constitute a major risk to students and to the aspirations of school systems for sustained improvements in mass education. It suggests that one of the major forms of managing the risks of the supply problem – succession planning – is critically important. However, succession planning, and strategies such as widening the scope of who can be school leaders, also produce a set of risks which require careful attention.

Chapter 1

Getting a head

The problem of supply

Most teachers become heads for idealistic reasons – they want to make a difference to the lives of children and young people. Most heads say that there are things about the job that they love – the contact with children and young people, and changing schools for the better. On a good day, there is no better job in the world.

But serving heads also suggest that the job is getting harder. Heads now talk openly at their professional conferences and to media about their discontent with policy, about high levels of stress and about leaving the job. There is concern about the shortage of applicants for leadership positions in the United States of America, Canada, Australia, New Zealand and the United Kingdom.[1] There are also difficulties in both teacher and headteacher supply in parts of Europe. It appears that it is not only increasingly difficult to fill at least some of 'the top jobs' but also that a significant number of young teachers do not see the job of school leadership/management as something they want to consider.

This chapter examines the 'supply problem' by considering its dimensions and the reasons that are generally given for the lack of applications. It covers a number of nations, and in doing so, runs the risk of glossing over some important differences. However my familiarity with the situation in England and Australia means that the bulk of the examples come from those two places. I have also concentrated on evidence which allows an international story to be told about supply.

How do we know there is a 'supply problem'?

There is a problem in trying to determine whether there is a problem of supply of applicants for headships! This is not only because there are not consistent frameworks for data collection across countries, but also in most cases, the data that exist within them are not regularly aggregated.

It is not always clear whose responsibility it is to collect information about headteachers. Federated countries such as the USA, Canada and Australia do not have comprehensive national occupational data systems and the information that is kept on heads is generally retained at the state/provincial level. In states/provinces where there are devolved systems of governance, data about heads might be kept at state, district/local authority and/or school level. Sometimes these data are aggregated and analysed and sometimes not. While some analysis on supply can be generated from census or pension statistics, most national supply data are generated via specific audits or surveys. This is the case in the UK. Thus, in order to understand the scope, scale and nature of supply of applicants for headship, it is necessary to consult a range of often very partial and incommensurate data sources.

There is also a question of access to data. Together with colleagues I attempted to research the supply problem in three states of Australia (Blackmore *et al.*, 2005). One state system refused to cooperate at all and the project had to be refocused on the two states that were prepared to be involved. The second state did not regularly collate data on how many jobs were advertised, who applied and what happened if the jobs were not filled. And because it had suffered severe cutbacks it had lost its sole workforce planner and could not quite yet afford the new human resources software system that would allow it to routinely predict trends in applications and shortages. Such analysis had to be undertaken as a specific 'project'. The third state was highly protective of its data, and refused to provide it on the grounds of its (political/industrial) sensitivity. However, another researcher had been able to access some of this material a year earlier. We argued in our project that these kinds of data were a matter of public interest and ought to be generally available (see also McNamara *et al.*, 2008; Owen *et al.*, 2008, on problems with workforce data).

Discussions about supply therefore are limited by the statistical data available. Nevertheless, there are *some* data, and what they suggest is that there is no problem of supply *per se.*

What do we know about the 'supply problem'?

There was considerable anxiety in the USA in the late 1990s and early 2000s about a shortage of applicants for headship. The National Association of Elementary School Principals and the National Association of Secondary Principals commissioned studies (Educational Research Service, 1998, 2000) which showed that school districts were finding it increasingly difficult to attract applicants for vacancies, while at the same time growing numbers of serving school leaders were retiring, taking important experience and expertise with them. Researchers took up the issue, focusing in the first instance on whether there was a 'crisis' and, if so, how it had been produced (e.g. Gilman and Lanman-Givens, 2001; Pounder and Merrill, 2001; Yerkes and Guaglianone, 1998).

After an initial debate about the size of the problem, US employers, professional associations and researchers stopped asking whether there was a general shortage and started asking whether there were specific schools and locations where it was easy to find people to apply for the post of head-teacher, and other locations and schools where it was almost impossible. One national study (Roza *et al.*, 2003) surveyed Directors of Human Resources and school superintendents, and conducted over 150 telephone interviews with district staff, school organizations and state officials. The researchers concluded that there was no overall problem with supply in the USA. In fact at the time, there were more people with the certification necessary to apply for headship than there were actual positions. Rather, they suggested, the problem was one of distribution. There were fewer applicants for schools and school districts where there were high concentrations of families on low incomes, racial isolation, low per-pupil budget allocations and low salaries. This combination also often coincided with poor test results in sites this study called 'the most challenging working conditions'. Districts with rapidly expanding populations also experienced some difficulty in filling posts, and secondary schools in general found it more difficult than primary to fill positions. On the other hand, rural school districts had less applicants for positions than city districts, but were relatively unconcerned about a crisis, since they tended to 'grow their own' leadership.

Other US researchers also reported distribution issues, reinforcing the notion that the difficulty lay in getting a range of suitable applicants for urban and other 'difficult' schools (Cooley and Shen, 2000; Kimball and Sirotnik, 2000; Pounder *et al.*, 2003). More recent US research suggests that teachers who already work in urban areas are not necessarily put off by the locality (Howley *et al.*, 2005), and there is some evidence that existing heads in urban areas are quite likely to apply for a second headship in a similar school (Militello and Behnke, 2006). This finding supports the idea that 'growing your own' schemes will be successful in these locations, although it could also be interpreted to mean that the lack of applications are for reasons other than 'challenge'.

Our Australian study came to a comparable conclusion – it was a matter of 'which school' not 'all schools' that had the supply problem. In Australia, 'which school' has its own distinctive locational twist (see Barty *et al.,* 2005). From our interviews with Directors of Human Resources, headteachers, tea-cher unions and District Superintendents, we concluded that there were few problems with the number of applications received by high fee independent schools, Catholic and other faith schools, medium-sized primary schools in metropolitan locations and schools in rural locations offering a desirable lifestyle. There were shortfalls in the number of applications for small pri-mary schools, most high schools and all schools serving low-income neigh-bourhoods. In the Australian context, rural and isolated schools, and most particularly those serving Aboriginal communities, had real difficulty in finding anyone to apply (see Box 1.1 for a UK comparison). However, while schools serving low-income communities received far fewer applications than

Box 1.1 Isolated schools have trouble getting heads[2]

With a pupil–teacher ratio of three-to-one, an impeccable discipline record and some of the most lavish learning resources in the country, on the face of it few pedagogues in their right mind would pass over the opportunity to work at Foula Primary School. The drawback, and of course there is one, is that the post of headteacher currently being advertised there could involve weeks trapped on the most northerly, fogbound and windswept island in Britain with only a handful of locals and the resident birdlife for company. To sweeten the pill, the job with Shetland Islands Council comes with a £41,742-a-year salary, plus a £2,000 remoteness allowance, a relocation package and a house. The current, part-time head, Fred Hibbert, who is stepping down when the role is merged with that of classroom teacher, said the successful candidate would have to be self-reliant.

'You are a long way away from help and some of the things you take for granted in a more usual setting you cannot take for granted here,' he said. There is no public transport, except off the island, while a punctured tyre can take three weeks to fix if the ferries are not working – which is often the case during the wild winters. The absence of a local shop means the weekly groceries have to be shipped or air-freighted in. This year's school roll is made up of just two boys, aged 10 and 3, while a third, their 3-year-old brother, will be joining them in August next year.

(http://news.independent.co.uk/education/education_news/article3260721. ece.; accessed 2 January 2008)

other schools, there were fewer reported concerns about the 'suitability and competence' of those who did apply. It seemed that in the two Australian states we studied there were still enough people committed to making a difference for children and young people at the 'bottom' of the social and economic barrel to fill available leadership positions. Questions of 'quality' were more an issue for those managing staffing in large secondary schools, where headteacher positions might be advertised several times before a suitable applicant was found.

Which-school-has-the-supply-problem takes another turn in England and Wales. John Howson's independent company, Education Data Services (EDS), has been conducting regular audits and surveys of the teacher and headteacher workforce for many years. Using public advertisements for leadership positions, follow-up surveys to see how many applications were received and how many positions were unfilled, and general surveys of heads, he has produced a body of public information which shows not only whether there appears to be problem in supply, but also where it is and how it has changed over time:

- In 2002, EDS reported that the total number of schools which failed to fill a head or deputy position was higher than at any previous time, although the number of headteacher vacancies was slightly lower than a couple of years previous. The situation was most acute in Church schools, schools in London and in rural areas, with schools in the Home Counties finding the least difficulty in getting their posts filled (Howson, 2002). These figures got steadily worse over the next few years.
- At the beginning of 2008, EDS reported that the number of secondary schools having to readvertise positions was lower than at any time since 2001/2002: re-advertisements ran at 25 per cent compared to 36 per cent for the previous two years. While an improvement, this was still one quarter of all of the 400 vacant posts where there was difficulty in finding a replacement. And the situation for primary schools had if anything got worse: 37 per cent of the 2,100 vacancies were unfilled the first time round, only a little better than the 38 per cent of 2004–5. The situation was most acute for faith schools, and schools in low-income parts of London, the north-west and the east of England and Wales (Howson, 2008).

EDS surveys suggest that in England the supply problem, taken to mean unfilled vacancies, is more acute for primary schools: there are more of them and the ratio of potential applicants to positions is lower than it is for secondary schools which are typically much larger in size and have more elaborate management structures.

The forecast for tomorrow is …

EDS surveys work with the situation in the immediate past. While this allows for some discussion of trends, more data is required to make accurate predictions of shortage. As noted, much of this material is not systematically and regularly collected. A specially commissioned study into the state of school leadership in England and Wales (Earley *et al.*, 2002) surveyed nearly 1500 heads, deputy and assistant heads and teachers undertaking leadership qualifications (the National Professional Qualification for Headship, the NPQH) in England. The report contained some important information:

> Six out of ten of the headteachers were planning to remain in their present post and four-in-ten were considering early retirement/retirement. Three out of ten included 'moving to another school' as a possible future work preference. Nearly two-thirds (63%) of NPQH candidates and over a quarter (27%) of the deputy/assistant head sample definitely wished to become headteachers. However, four out of ten deputy/assistant heads

stated that they had no plans to become a head. Most of those wanting to become headteachers, or to move on to another headship, would prefer to go to a school which was not in a challenging situation.

(ibid., p. 7)

A follow-up study (Stevens *et al.*, 2005) of over 1000 schools conducted two years later reported some changes to this picture:

Half of [the] headteachers say they envisage leaving their current school in the next three years, typically because they are retiring or seeking a headship in a different school. The majority of those headteachers who seek a headship elsewhere would be prepared to work in a school in challenging circumstances ... The proportion of middle leaders who would like to become deputy headteachers and/or headteachers has increased since 2001. Three in ten middle leaders say it is their aim to be a headteacher at some stage, the drivers being job satisfaction/sense of personal achievement, maintaining high standards and rising to a new challenge, with the preference being to become a headteacher in a coasting school (one showing little progress), non-selective school or rural school.

(ibid., pp. 1–2)

The willingness of serving heads to take up posts in schools that serve low-income neighbourhoods is significant (this may also be something that has recently changed in England, see Chapter 7). The data from this study do suggest that there will be problems in supply in the future, with a significant number – seven out of ten middle leaders – unwilling to take on headship at all, with those who *are* keen more likely to apply for a comfortable position.

Howson suggests that more 'supply' research is needed:

We still do not know enough about the actions of those seeking headships: how many posts do they apply for at any one time, how far afield are they prepared to look and what types of school will they consider.

(Howson, 2008, p. 14)

This is not all. We need to know more about how many applications are received for positions that are filled and those that are readvertised, from whom and the reasons for their choices. We also need to know much more about the processes of selection (of this, more later).

But despite these statistical difficulties and caveats, it is safe to say there *is* a body of literature which suggests that, in the West, the 'supply problem' has distinctive geographies which are tied to the socio-political-economic circumstances of specific localities and populations and the size and reputations of schools.

Why is there a supply problem?

The first and most obvious reason for the supply problem is demographic. The post-war population growth in Western nations, popularly known as the baby boom, produced a demand for many more schools. Rapid expansion in the number of schools saw a large cohort of teachers become school leaders/ managers. That cohort is now reaching retirement age.

Not shy, but certainly retiring

In England and Wales the high point for retirement is predicted to be 2009 but with a 'problem' on either side of this date. In 2007, the National College for School Leadership noted:

> Nearly a quarter of heads are aged over 55, and as they retire over the next 5 years, the profession will be deprived of a great swathe of experienced leaders. At the same time, too few new leaders are putting themselves forward.
>
> (National College for School Leadership, 2007, p. 5)

In 2008, the College had become even more alarmed by the demographic inevitabilities:

> Up to 55% of headteachers could retire within four years according to the government's chief adviser on school leadership who says that schools are facing a demographic 'time bomb' in the staff room. Some schools may consider employing heads who have no experience of teaching in order to fill posts, said Steve Mumby, head of the National College for School Leadership (NCSL). Official figures suggest that half of head-teachers will retire in 10 years but internal research conducted by the NCSL reveals that the figure could be much higher. Up to 55% are due for retirement or could leave if current trends continue by 2012 ... A bulge in the number of headteachers about to turn 60 – fuelled by the 1950s baby-boomer generation – is behind the problem.
>
> (*Education Guardian*, 19 June 2008)

However, the situation is complicated by what in cash-strapped times appears as a very generous pension (or superannuation) scheme which has allowed many to retire well before they are 60. Despite the age of retirement being increased to 65 and part-time employment being made more finan-cially attractive, there is little financial incentive for many to remain as heads. Indeed, the number of leaders retiring before they turn 60 far exceeds that of those who retire at or after 60, although there is a suggestion that the proclivity for early retirement might be changing with modifications to the pension scheme (Peters *et al.*, 2008). This demographic and pension nexus has its equivalents in Canada, Australia and New Zealand and the United States (Costrell and Podursky, 2007), although the actual year when retirement peaks varies from country to country.

As the baby boomers retire, there is an accompanying need for larger numbers of teachers to enter the system (Darling-Hammond and Sykes, 2003; Preston, 2001). Significant issues of teacher supply are reported in Europe and in the United States, Canada, Australia and New Zealand. In the United Kingdom, studies of teacher shortages have revealed that, just as is the case with headteachers, the situation is not simply one of supply, but is rather a matter of shortfalls in specific disciplines, and issues attached to particular locations (Gorard *et al.*, 2007; see White and Smith, 2005, for an international picture). In English inner cities, for example, many schools face extreme difficulties in finding enough teachers to fill positions and must rely on a steady stream of young overseas trained teachers, ironically often from countries also experiencing teacher shortages (Macbeath *et al.*, 2007).

But the problem with the teacher shortage is that it is not simply about getting someone warm, upright and halfway decent in post – it is also about keeping them there. A national survey of around 2,500 English teachers reported that: 'Some projected that they would leave the teaching profession within the next five years: 29 per cent planned to retire; 15 per cent planned to move to employment outside of teaching; and 12 per cent planned to take a career break' (General Teaching Council for England, 2008, p. 4). The General Teaching Council concluded that retention of teachers was a serious issue and noted its flow-on effects into school leadership/management.

Demographic 'black holes' in the supply of heads cannot simply be attributed to the financial incentives to retire and a lack of teacher applicants. Research suggests that there are other issues at stake.

A case of premature evacuation?

The issues that are reported to affect headteacher supply are numerous. These are broadly reported as being: the unrealistic expectations put on heads, the changing nature of the work, the remuneration offered and the effects of headship on family and lifestyle.

Table 1.1 shows a comparison of three analyses of the shortage – Dorman and D'Arbon's (2003a) report of a study of shortages in Australian Catholic schools which includes issues of location and faith and omits macro-social concerns and teacher supply; Macbeath's (2006b) internationally focused literature-based study; and Mulford's (2003) study for the OECD which contains much more detail about the changing nature of head-teacher's work both at systemic and school level. Mulford also includes as a factor the industrial/professional relationships between education systems and their teachers.

Table 1.1 Reasons for the supply shortages

Dorman and D'Arbon (2003a)	Macbeath (2006b)	Mulford (2003)
Increasing demands of society on the personal and professional life and time commitment of the principal	Social factors Workload Unrelenting change Stress	Societal problems (poverty, inadequate health care, unemployment); Unrelenting change; increasing and sometimes conflicting expectations. A feeling that education is an economic and political football in which those in schools are not valued. The job is too demanding, conflictual, stressful, deskilling, lonely, isolated, separated from teaching, lacking support, unrewarding
Increasing responsibilities of the position	Changing nature of school leadership Unrelenting change Intensification Competition Accountablity and bureaucracy	An emphasis on administration rather than leadership. Mandates and accountability (such as curriculum and/or priority programmes, high stakes testing, performance management). Bureaucracy (especially excessive paper work, the increase in intermediate bodies and new approaches such as whole-of government). Competition. A conspiracy of busyness, that is, the way time, space and communication patterns are structured. Declining authority to act. Budget cuts. Overcrowding Poor employer/professional educator relations
Lifestyle issues, especially those related to balancing personal (e.g. family) and professional expectations	Personal and domestic concerns. Workload Stress	Long hours
Gender concerns, especially those related to women's perceptions of their accessibility to the principalship	Personal and domestic concerns	The job is only for particular groups in society
Income concerns	Salary Selection	Teaching as a low-ceiling career
Recruitment pathways to the principalship		
City and country placement issues		
Disruption to family life by relocation to take up a new position	Personal and domestic concerns	
Transition from 'religious' model to 'lay' model of school leadership	Changing nature of school leadership	
	Teacher supply line	Teacher shortages

These factors are not equally significant for all heads. For example, some worry about pay more than others. Smithers and Robinson (2006) conducted a study of school leadership for the National Union of Teachers (UK). They found that salary was particularly an issue for some primary headteachers:

> Three-quarters of primary schools reported having teachers with the qualities to become a headteacher but who did not want to move up. Nearly two-thirds of the primary heads thought that this was because the pay differential was not a sufficient incentive. The heads of small schools complained that at the top of their scale they would be receiving less than a deputy of a larger school or the second in a department in a secondary school.
>
> (ibid., p. iii)

Some researchers (e.g. Whitaker, 2003) suggest that the most significant disincentive for applicants arises from the changes in the role and work of headship. But the Australian Catholic education study led by D'Arbon proposed that:

> [B]oth men and women in primary and secondary indicated that the impact of the principalship on personal and family life ranked first in importance. All, except females in secondary schools, ranked 'an unsupportive external environment' as the second strongest perception. This referred to a lack of support from, for example, the community, the central office of the system, as well as more critical parents and the media.
>
> (D'Arbon *et al.*, 2002, p. 476)

A study conducted in England and Wales (Stevens *et al.*, 2005) reported that:

> A quarter of deputies hope to become headteachers within the next three years. The main drivers of this ambition are the opportunity to build shared values and job satisfaction/personal achievement. Stress, personal priorities and less frequent contact with pupils are the major disincentives of taking on the post of headteacher.
>
> (ibid., p. 2)

These studies (see also Cranston, 2007; Kruger *et al.*, 2001, 2005) suggest that the problem for existing and potential heads is the ways in which expectations, the role and the actual work in specific school contexts play out in quality of life family relationships, well-being and health. There are also professional impacts on commitment to teaching and to personal relationships with students, staff and families.

Supply – what's in a name?

The language of supply, posts, vacancies and quality masks an important reality. International studies of headship and of shortages of applicants show distinctive patterns which are produced from the interplay of gender, race and ethnicity and disability.

Schools in Western countries are overwhelmingly run by white administrators. This is the legacy of raced institutional practices which allow limited numbers of people ascribed with 'minority heritage' to become teachers. In January 2007, for example, government statistics for England and Wales reported:

> 94.6 per cent of teachers in the white ethnic groups, a decrease of 0.2 percentage points from 2006; the Mixed/Dual group provided 0.7 per cent of the total in 2007, the same as in 2006; the Asian or Asian British group provided 2.4 per cent of the total in 2007, an increase from 2.2 per cent in 2006; the Black or Black British group provided 1.7 per cent of the total in 2007, the same as in 2006. The increase in the percentage of teachers from minority ethnic (non-white) groups was greater in the London region, 17.9 per cent in 2007, compared to 17.4 per cent in 2006.
>
> (DfES, 2007, p. 2)

This is well below the 9 per cent that 'ethnic minority' groups contribute to the overall English population. Until the teaching profession is more diverse, then it is unlikely that the composition of the leadership cohort will change significantly.

Teachers with 'other' identities and knowledges do not always find it easy to make their way up the career 'ladder'. Headteacher certification and professional development programmes often pay token attention to questions of race (Rusch, 2004), while the apparently neutral policy discourses of effectiveness and improvement push social and cultural questions to the background (Rassool and Morley, 2000). The National College for School Leadership (NCSL) in England, however, has commissioned research (Bush *et al.*, 2005) into the needs of serving and aspiring ethnic and minority leaders and does run a dedicated programme for what it calls 'EM leaders' (Ethnic Minority). Promotion, recruitment and appointment practices can also subtly advantage white applicants (Powney *et al.*, 2003). Menter and his colleagues (Menter *et al.*, 2003), for example, found evidence that headteachers in England and Wales were reluctant to favourably assess teachers who were not white in promotion processes. But experiences of racism vary substantively from place to place. While English heads report subtle forms of discrimination, Black heads in South Africa report overt racism from white communities, a direct legacy of the long years of Apartheid (Moloi and Potgieter, 2006).

Those headteachers with minority race and ethnic heritages who do 'get through the system' are often concentrated in schools with large numbers of students with minority and ethnic heritages. This concentration is borne from the commitments of headteacher applicants wanting to make a difference in, with and for their own communities, and in many cases a stated preference by those recruiting and appointing for applicants who will act as 'role models' for students (Brown, 2004; Dantley, 2003; Eilers and Camacho, 2007). Ironically, the expertise, knowledge and experiences of those who do 'make it' against the odds are often ignored in the literatures on school leadership (Ah Nee-Benham and Cooper, 1998; Bloom and Erlandson, 2003; Johnson, 2006; Murtadha and Watts, 2005), as are detailed studies of White head-teachers who confront racism (Evans, 2007; Jansen, 2006).

Whiteness is not the only case of disproportionate representation in the headship. The ratio of men and women in headteacher positions is not the same as their proportion in the teaching workforce. Primary schools are over-whelmingly female, and while there are now more female than male head-teachers, they numerically lag behind their ratio within the primary workforce. The situation is much more severe in secondary schools where men over-whelmingly dominate leadership/management positions:

- In 2002, Earley and colleagues (Earley *et al.*, 2002, p. 24) cite total head-teacher figures for England and Wales of 47.5 per cent male and 52.5 per cent female.
- Three years later, the NCSL reported that 31 per cent of secondary heads and deputies were women, while in the largest secondary schools a whopping 85 per cent of headteachers were male (Coleman, 2005).
- In 2007, the DfES (Department for Education and Skills, 2007, p. 123) reported that 35 per cent of secondary female heads were drawn from 56 per cent of the total teaching workforce, noting that male teachers were 'more likely' to be promoted to headteacher.

This gender imbalance may not get much better very quickly. A national teacher survey in England in 2007 (cf. Dorman and D'Arbon, 2003b, in Australia) concluded that 'a higher percentage of men (41 per cent) than women (29 per cent) anticipated moving into management posts other than headship, and men were twice as likely as women to envisage becoming a head teacher' (General Teaching Council for England, 2008, p. 4).

While it is the case that the proportion of women in senior positions has increased over time, and while figures vary from place to place, the picture of unequal female participation in leadership is generally true and shows little evidence of changing rapidly (Blackmore, 1999; Coleman, 2005).

The reasons for women's lower participation in headship include the following:

- family responsibilities;
- lack of opportunity to gain leadership experience;

- discrimination in selection and appointment procedures;
- allocation of stereotypical leadership roles.

Family responsibilities

The need to look after children constrains women in particular, despite a trend for more men to take advantage of parenting leave provisions. The provision of childcare and more responsive leave are necessary but not sufficient to cover parenting and caring responsibilities and the inadequacies do affect career progression. Coleman (2005, p. 3) reports that, in England:

> [S]ome women have had to make choices between their careers and domestic life. The proportion of female secondary headteachers with children is higher than it was in the 1990s (60 per cent compared to 50 per cent). However, female secondary headteachers remain far less likely to have children than their male colleagues (60 per cent compared to 90 per cent). Female headteachers from all sectors are also still more likely to be single, divorced or separated than their male counterparts.

Coleman also suggests that it is often the male partner whose job mobility dictates location and opportunity.

But the issue of family responsibilities plays out differently for different groups of women. Women of different 'generations' have various calls on them, and may cope differently; the support structures available to them may also be culturally and locationally inflected. Loder's study of 31 American headteachers (Loder, 2005, p. 741), for example, shows that:

> [W]omen in the 'older' generation were compelled to prioritize family above professional pursuits more so than women in the 'younger' generation ... Black administrators relied on extended women kinship ties for child care and household support whereas White administrators primarily sought spousal support.

As well, women are variously positioned by the demands of their particular schools and communities (Smulyan, 2000) with some much more demanding of after hours and early morning work than others.

Lack of opportunity to gain leadership experience

Women teachers advance more slowly through the promotion 'ladder'.

> [Some] 20% of male primary teachers with 5–9 years of service are already on the Leadership Scale compared with 8.5% of women ... in the secondary sector 3.5% of male teachers with 5–9 years of service are on the

Leadership Scale compared with 2% of women ... in special schools after 5–9 years of service 10% of men are already on the Leadership Scale compared with 6% of women.

(McNamara *et al.*, 2008, p. ii)

These data suggest that men are more likely to be talent spotted by senior managers, put themselves forward for promotion and acting opportunities, and/or that career planning practices within schools covertly favour men (Draper and McMichael, 1998; Kidd *et al.*, 2004). This phenomenon requires further investigation. The end result is that women are disproportionately left behind in the promotion stakes from the very outset of their careers.

Discrimination in selection and appointment procedures

Brooking's (2004) investigation of the practices of autonomous school boards in New Zealand shows alarming levels of discrimination during selection (see also Court, 1998). Narrow job descriptions were combined with overt sexism in questioning. 'The ability to discipline was discursively constructed as a male attribute by school boards, and was frequently positioned as opposi- tional to "women's leadership styles".' According to Brooking:

Gender didn't come into it. Well, OK, the discipline thing, her size and that type of thing probably would have counted against her with dealing with some of the characters we've got. Some of the board did have 'we want a man, no matter what' attitude, but the process we went through to appoint, we had just the person that we wanted (Board chair of small school with male principal: Int 15, p. 3).

(Brooking, 2004, p. 211)

Our Australian study of selection panels (Blackmore *et al.*, 2006) found much the same, with selection panel preferences for experience and a 'safe pair of hands' transforming into decisions to appoint the (male) *status quo*. We were told by frustrated applicants of expectations of coaching the local football team (rural school) and the need for strong father role-models (inner city school). In one instance the local hotel took bets on how long the newly appointed female head would stay (isolated school) – she outlasted all previous male appoint- ments by some years (see also Sherman, 2000, in rural Canada).

Allocation of stereotypical leadership roles

It is less likely to be the case now than in the past that women are identified with pastoral responsibilities and men with curriculum, timetabling and evaluation. Coleman (undated, p. 4) notes: 'There appears to have been some reduction in the amount of gender stereotyping that takes place in secondary schools in recent years.' This trend places women in a better position to match the experience requirements of job descriptions, and also influences the ways in which those on selection panels view the applicants. Nevertheless, our Australian study of co-principalship revealed highly gendered patterns of responsibility (Thomson and Blackmore, 2006), and it is clear that the hard/soft administrative binary is still alive.

There are some very notable exceptions to the general gendered pattern of headship. One is in the Australian state where I was a headteacher. When I formally became a member of the South Australian Secondary Principals Association in 1984, there were three other women members. By the time I resigned as President of the Association in 1996, women comprised 42 per cent of the membership. Some five years later, this number had climbed to 50 per cent. This situation was achieved through the capacities of state equal opportunity legislation (see Blackmore and Sachs, 2007; Yeatman, 1990, for an explanation of the distinctive Australian approach to equity via public sector reform). Through application for specific legally described exemptions, public sector organizations were allowed to determine that a job was only for women or for Indigenous or ethnic minority applicants. In the state education system, the exemption was directed to two positions – female Deputies in schools where there were no other women in the senior management team, and female Physical Education teachers where there were no other women with that specialization on staff. The exemption was primarily applied to vacancies in secondary schools. The result was that over time, a pool of women secondary Deputies were created. Because they had the relevant experience, they were then able to successfully compete for headteacher positions. This section of the Act has now been repealed.

This example points to the importance of carefully planned interventions in the 'supply problem', a matter to which I return in the next chapter. It also reinforces the point that supply is not simply a question of geography and demography and concerns about work and lifestyle. It is also a matter of who applies and the barriers that might be in their way.

Further complications in the supply line

One US study of supply (Roza *et al.*, 2003) concluded that notions of a general shortage of applicants were based on a set of myths passed from one person and organization to another:

> The conventional wisdom about principal shortages appears to be self-reinforcing, a phenomenon built on troubling anecdotes, a belief that the quality of today's candidates does not match that of yesterday's, and a conviction that the leadership demands on today's principal require more highly-capable candidates.
>
> (Roza *et al.*, 2003, p. 11)

These researchers proposed that the myths of shortage masked an issue about the quality and suitability of applicants. Getting a head wasn't just about how many people applied, they said, but whether there were applicants who were capable of doing the job.

Those who study supply agree that anecdotes about the difficulties of attracting 'quality' applicants are on the increase, but there is actually very little research into the reality. Perhaps the number of readvertised vacancies reported through the EDS annual study (e.g. Howson, 2008) is evidence of a quality problem, since it is unlikely that there were no applications at all for all of the unfilled posts.

But the question of capability and quality is vexed. It not only raises concerns about who decides that applicants either do or don't possess 'the right stuff', but also:

- what counts as quality;
- whether this version of quality advantages some people and not others, and if so how;
- who is responsible for monitoring the efficacy and parity of processes used for selection of competency and quality;
- who is responsible for monitoring the equity of the individual and cumulative processes of appointment.

Even if there may or may not be a quality problem in reality, there is certainly a quality dilemma. One response to the quality dilemma is to address the point of application. The development of headteacher standards and training and assessment procedures are systemic attempts to create a satisfactory 'quality' base-line. There is considerable debate in the USA (Donmoyer, 1999; Donmoyer *et al.*, 1995; English, 2000, 2006; Murphy, 2005) and in England (Bright and Ware, 2003; Earley *et al.*, 2002; Gunter, 1999) about the very notion of standards, how they are developed and by whom, and the utility of the certification education that they support. Standards, like tests, are said to privilege a static and relatively narrow and 'observable' set of behaviours which fail to provide school leaders with the kinds of deep knowledge resources that they need (English, 2008). However, standards *per se* are not the major focus of this book: there are other texts that do this job.

This book is primarily concerned with the question of supply in relation to the disincentives for teachers to apply and serving heads to stay. The provision of training and professional development *is*, however, discussed throughout the text.

Supply in a nutshell

This chapter has argued that the shortage of applicants for headteachers' positions is not universal. Rather there are shortages in particular locations, types and sizes of schools. Shortages of applicants are a product of demographic change in the form of retirements, but also of the reluctance of significant numbers of teachers to consider the headship *and* of serving headteachers to stay till they are 60, now 65. There is also cultural homogeneity among those in leadership positions and a significant gender bias is still evident across the leadership cohort. Some unfilled headteacher vacancies might also arise because applicants are not perceived to be of sufficient 'quality'.

Supply constitutes a significant risk for schools and for the education system. It is a risk which must be managed; it cannot be avoided. The potential harm to students of having large numbers of senior leaders leave at around the same time must be minimized. In order to manage this risk, education systems are banking on succession planning as their major risk management strategy.

Chapter 2

A heads up

Solutions to the supply problem

There is no single and simple answer to the question, 'How do teachers decide to become headteachers?' Research suggests that while some enter the teaching profession with the view that they want to have the 'top job', others do not. They form that view because they are working in a school with a good headteacher and decide that the job is for them. They decide to go for promotion because a significant senior leader has suggested it to them, or because they have been 'talent spotted' and mentored (Baskwill, 2003; Bright and Ware, 2003; Daresh and Male, 2000; Ribbins, 1999). But working in a school where there is a less than stellar head also provokes some to think that they could do the job better (Sieber, undated). Some teachers take up advisory positions where they get a more expansive view of schooling (McKenley and Gordon, 2002) and many have headship thrust on them through 'acting' in the role when a head suddenly leaves (Draper and McMichael, 2003).

In a study of 145 mainly primary heads and aspiring heads, Bright and Ware (2003, p.8) found that:

> the typical primary head had spent five years as a deputy while some of her colleagues skipped that stage entirely and others dwelt there for some considerable time – 26 years in one case before finally taking the plunge into headship. She had previously combined the roles of deputy head and classroom teacher. She gained her first headship at the age of 39, and although a few of her colleagues achieved that promotion early in their careers, 26 being the youngest, one colleague took on the challenges of headship at the age of 56, an age when many in the profession are already looking forward to retirement.

They suggest that 'there is an incredible range and diversity in routes to headship with little or no suggestion of a particular career path or paths' (see Box 2.1).

The fact that there is no universal pathway to headship means that addressing the 'supply problem' is difficult. Policy makers must develop a menu of interventions which attempt to address the multiple pathways taken

Box 2.1 Sandra: one route to headship

[W]hen you're a little girl you think that you're going to be a teacher, and once I was a teacher, I was going to be a head. I didn't think it would happen but I worked towards it and I made sure that I sought out posts with good heads and that's the best training you can get. When I first went back to work full-time after having the girls, I had a curriculum development post and I heard this job was coming up and I would have died for it even though it was in an Infants school and I'd never taught infants in my life. But I really wanted to work with this woman and I had four fantastic years there and I was like a sponge. Everything that I could possibly take from her I did. I then went for a deputy headship with another very dynamic head and both of them always had the community – the school community – as part of everything they did. Nothing could have replaced that for me. I mean, I did the NPQH but I don't know what that did for me but I went through the process and did it. But it's not an appropriate form of training for a job like this. You need to live and breathe that work with people who have already got those skills.

(Sandra, Primary head, UK)

by future heads, rather than opt for a universal approach. Regardless of what is done, all policy interventions designed to address the 'supply problem' must take on board the understanding that becoming a head is in part a process of socialization (Crow, undated) into particular ways of being and acting. Deciding to become a headteacher is in part a decision to become someone other than a classroom teacher, and to claim expertise, authority and power in relation to the education of children and young people. This 'identity' issue is an important aspect of supply: prospective applicants must be able to *see themselves* in the position while also being able to identify important *continuities* between their teacherly identity/ies and that of headteacher. Sandra's statements in Box 2.1 provide a helpful example of headteacher identity formation.

Holland and colleagues (Holland *et al.*, 1998) argue that identity formation occurs in a given community of practice. They argue that the self is always 'authored', that is it is produced via active agency in iterative relation to structure, which they call a 'figured world'. They say:

> The self is a position from which meaning is made, a position that is 'addressed' by and 'answers' others and the 'world' (the physical and cultural environment). In answering (which is the stuff of existence), the self 'authors' the world – including itself and others.

(ibid., p. 173)

They suggest that identity formation goes through four authoring stages:

1 Identity devaluation, in which a new understanding of self develops at the expense of an old one – Sandra decided to move from teacher to headteacher.
2 Personalization of the identity, through identification with key figures – Sandra identified with outstanding heads she chose to work with.
3 Emotional attachment to the new identity – Sandra saw herself as a headteacher and came to understand herself and her actions as being that of headteacher.
4 Identity reconstitution, through exorcising negative practices – Sandra formed a strong sense of moral purpose about the kinds of good practice she needed to head up in her school (see more of Sandra's story in Chapter 7).

This framing suggests that any process of becoming a headteacher, no matter how different, needs to take account of each of these identity formation stages.

In this chapter, I examine some succession planning schemes that are on offer and, using risk and its management as a lens, I consider four risks which underpin succession planning as 'the solution' to the 'supply problem'. I begin by unpicking the ways in which the 'supply problem' is conceptualized. I conclude by noting other related interventions.

Getting a grip on problems and solutions

The way in which problems are analysed and understood anticipates and produces specific kinds of solutions. Every problem does not just have *a* solution, it has *the* particular solution(s) envisaged in the way the problem has been understood (Bacchi, 1999).

Take the 'supply problem' and the lack of women applicants for headship. The policy solution for the gender imbalance in headship will be determined by whether it is understood as:

- a problem with the women themselves – they don't apply because they don't have the confidence/skills;
- a problem for the women – they can't apply because they have other competing commitments; or
- the problem is the lack of 'fit' between the criteria and the women – they don't apply because they haven't had the opportunity to have the appropriate experiences, or the knowledge which women are likely to have had are not included in job requirements, or the post's criteria value a narrow set of experiences which rule women out.

Depending on which problematization is favoured, a different policy solution will be produced – a 'no confidence' analysis leads to assertiveness training;

'competing commitments' leads to policies related to families; 'lack of appropriate experience' leads to shadowing and acting positions; 'narrow criteria' leads to revised job descriptions and appointment procedures. Mentoring and coaching tend to be offered for both lack of confidence and lack of experience. It is important to note that in this example some problem–solutions are training oriented, while other problem–solutions work through changing policy.

The mix of policy and training identified in relation to gender applies more generally to the supply issue. Table 2.1 represents the policy solutions that are offered to most of the problems that are associated with supply. The solutions menu – a balance of training and policy – can be found in the vast majority of countries with a recognized supply problem.

One solution that does not appear in Table 2.1 is that related to the teacher supply line. This is because tackling headteacher shortages via teacher supply is a high-risk strategy. Unless there is tightly controlled central management of supply and demand, simply training more teachers can quickly create a costly oversupply in particular locations while not resolving the shortages in 'unpopular' ones. There are then knock-on effects: widespread disillusionment among trained but under-employed teachers which acts as a disincentive for

Table 2.1 Common approaches to the supply problem

Problem	Solution
Lack of applicants	Policy about the recruitment practices of governors and school boards. Training for governors.
	Succession planning (in and out of school programmes, see later this chapter)
	Talent spotting schemes
	'Fast track' promotion schemes
	Mentoring
Shortage in specific locations	'Grow your own' schemes
	Location incentive allowances
	Higher salaries
Income concerns	Higher salaries
The role	New organizational forms of headship (see Chapter 8)
	New administrative support structures in large schools that can afford them
Workload	Managing work/life balance programmes (see Chapter 8)
	Stress management
	New administrative support structures in large schools that can afford them
Lack of women and ethnic minority applicants	Targeted training
	A policy of, and training about 'management of diversity' and training for line managers and employing bodies
Lack of quality	Standards
	Assessment centres
	Certification

the most highly qualified graduates to enter the profession and this in turn depresses the entry levels for teacher education programmes. By the time permanent jobs become available for them, young teachers have found other careers which they then do not leave. This syndrome is well known in Australia where the supply–demand–quality balance was out of kilter from the mid-1980s to the early 1990s.

This instance is instructive because it demonstrates that some solutions can produce undesirable outcomes. There can also be unanticipated outcomes and these arise when the context changes, and/or when the way that a problem is understood and the solution that is implemented are inadequate. One clear example of an unanticipated outcome is the way in which in the desegregation of US schools, intended to be of benefit to White and Black students, removed Black school headteachers from their posts and from the school system (Karpinski, 2006). The risk of removing particular types of school leaders is inherent to *all* schemes of school restructuring, but is rarely considered as one of the possible consequences.

Succession planning is a major plank in any cogent strategy to address the risks inherent in the 'supply problem'. It seems obvious that working without any succession planning at all is a seriously risky business. Doing nothing systematic relies entirely on the vagaries and serendipities of circumstance. Some headteachers might offer leadership opportunities to teachers, others might not. Some teachers might avail themselves of professional development, others might not. Some inner-city locations might attract enough applicants, others might not. Yet some schools and states do not have serious succession planning strategies in place.

Succession planning: tackling the 'supply problem' head on

In 2001, researchers from the Shriver Center, a cooperative venture established in Greater Baltimore, Maryland, USA to improve educational participation in the inner city, examined what they called a 'serious educational crisis'. They predicted that by 2005, two-thirds of all Maryland headteachers would be eligible to retire. Furthermore, they suggested, many existing headteachers did not intend to stay until they were of retirement age because they were experiencing 'too little compensation, too much stress, and too many hours' (Breedon *et al.*, 2001, p. 2). The researchers suggested that the certification requirements restricted the number of people who were eligible to apply for headship and argued that a more open system was required.

The policy answer was to institute a county-based, two-year principal preparatory seminar which would educate interested applicants on 'the supervision of teachers, the coordination of school activities and programmes, special education services, counselling of students and administrative paperwork' (ibid., p. 2). The seminar would be taught by county officials and 'high quality principals', would consist of workshops, seminars and a mentorship, would meet national standards, and would work cooperatively with higher education institutions and professional associations. Applicants, now renamed 'novice' heads would be placed in schools (or remain in their own) for a two-year internship under the daily supervision of the existing head, after which they would be eligible for appointment to their own school. This proposal was modelled on a scheme already in operation in Kentucky, which the researchers judged to be the most 'comprehensive, beneficial and practical' in the country. The researchers particularly noted the benefits of aspiring heads being able to 'learn the specifics and regulations of the county in which they plan to become principal' (ibid., p. 5) (see also Box 2.2).

Internship is one example of the way in which the 'supply problem' is addressed. It is not only expansive, but also expensive, and thus something which is relatively rare among succession strategies. Nevertheless, and as already noted, most school systems do have some kind of succession planning scheme in place. These generally include two elements:

1 an out-of-school training programme;
2 in-school experience.

An out-of-school training programme

Prospective applicants are brought together to form a supportive 'cohort'. Input from experienced headteachers and/or academics is combined with case study/problem-based work and some individual school-based projects.

There are different ways of constructing this experience:

- Where national standards for headship have been developed, there is more thorough external provision.

Box 2.2 Internship-based preparation

The Aspiring Principals program run by Dennis Littky of Rhode Island's Big Picture Company helps train aspiring principals by partnering them in a one-year apprenticeship with a distinguished principal from one of the nation's best small schools. Apprentice principals shadow distinguished principals as they do their job, observing and learning. While there is an academic component with the aspiring principals and certification from a college, the bulk of the program is hands on work and projects ... The organisation continues to maintain contact with its graduates, forming a network of principals who share information with each other.

(National Staff Development Council, undated, p. 13)

- Some US states require heads to have accredited higher education degrees and this provision is complemented by state-provided professional development.
- In England, the National Professional Qualification for Headship (NPQH) is mandatory for all aspiring heads and is provided through the National College for School Leadership.
- In Australia and New Zealand, there is some systemic professional development but nothing is mandated as a prerequisite. The Catholic Education systems in Australia have funded their school leaders to undertake Masters programmes and this is now a nearly universal qualification without it having to be mandated.

In the USA, assessment centres may form part of the out-of-school provision. They are also often used as means of selecting potential headteachers to go into a 'pool' from which interns, acting heads and new heads can be drawn. Assessment centre technologies require applicants to undertake in-basket activities, a group task and some kind of presentation. These activities are particularly good at showing who does not have the interpersonal practices or very basic organizational skills to undertake the work of running a school. Assessment centre participants are observed throughout the exercises, which can take up to three days, and they are given feedback on their performance. The experience is designed to assist prospective headteachers to develop a bespoke professional development programme to address their weaknesses. In cases where school systems have paid for participation in assessment centres, results are also given to the funder where they may preclude some people from promotion, and fast track others.[1]

In-school experience

'Growing your own' leadership is accomplished in single schools or clusters of schools. Hartley and Thomas (2005) identity what they call the school 'leadership pipeline' – a six-step approach to leadership talent development: (1) create a culture for growth; (2) benchmark current practice; (3) define the leadership qualities required; (4) identify the leadership talent pool; (5) assess individual talent; and (6) grow leadership talent. In practice, this means instituting an expanded set of formal leadership positions, systematic use of 'acting up' procedures, the distribution of opportunities to lead and manage school development programmes and projects, and formal processes of professional growth planning (Harris, 2008). The Australian Principals Associations Professional Development Centre (APAPDC) has had federal funding to develop models of 'good practice' in succession planning and the NCSL has a 'greenhouse schools' programme (National College for School Leadership, 2007). 'Executive' heads to federations of schools in England may provide new heads of component schools with something like an 'internship' experience. These are all 'grow your own' schemes.

But there is variation in the degree to which serving headteachers take succession planning seriously and there are many schools where opportunities to build a leadership career are very *ad hoc*, rather than being the result of a systematic approach to staff 'capacity building'. However, most new heads do get their hands-on experience of the top job from periods of 'acting up' when they do the job of head in the real head's absence. Researchers (Draper and McMichael, 2003) have found that acting heads have inadequate preparation and little support when they are in the role. They have to 'sink or swim' and face a difficult task in maintaining a school in which they have no mandate to initiate any change. This can act as a deterrent to their desire to take the job on 'for real'. These are issues which threaten an holistic approach to redressing the supply problem, and they are evidence of the fragility of succession planning.

Succession planning as risk management

If succession planning is a major risk management strategy, it is also one which runs risks which can be minimized, but are unlikely to be avoidable in some form. There are four major risks inherent in most succession planning.

Risky assumption I: Potential leaders can be identified

The succession literature is replete with the notion of identifying leadership talent. Headteachers are urged to ensure that they have human resources policies and personnel to ensure 'consistent understanding of the characteristics of leadership talent and leadership potential amongst staff' (Rhodes *et al.*, 2006). However, there is actually very little investigation of what it is that 'talent spotters' look for, but perhaps it is, as Barker (2003) suggests, a conjunction of qualities – showing empathy, possessing an aura, being reflective practitioners, having a realistic self-belief and drive, and being astute.

Despite the lack of debate about what constitutes 'leadership potential' the succession literature does assume that it is possible to recognize it. It also assumes that everyone will see the same things in the same people (but see Box 2.2). Two of the issues related to 'talent spotting' are:

1 *What is meant by talent?* 'Talent spotting' is spoken about by succession planners as if identification were straightforward and not replete with all the contingencies and inequities attached to any judgement. Given the possibility of 'cloning' – that is the tendency for people to select people just like themselves (Baker and Cooper, 2005; Gronn and Lacey, 2006) – that exists in the processes of leadership development, the very idea of talent spotting raises questions: Who decides what counts as talent, and how that might be determined? Does the teacher who takes the sports team after school have more 'self-drive' than the teacher who has to rush away to collect their own children from after school care? Is 'an aura' a

culturally specific way of speaking and behaving? Who decides about 'empathy' – someone watching or the person(s) to whom it is offered? What behaviours don't count as talent?

2   *The importance of context.* To show talent, one must be in a situation where there is opportunity to do so. So for example, for teachers to show empathy they must be working in a situation where this is encouraged. Empathy is not an innate quality but learned and practised. 'Walking in another's shoes' has cognitive components as well as emotional. And, like all acting/learning in organizations, empathy is something that is found happening between people, rather than within each one. If empathy is desirable, then it must be part of the informal and formal learning that goes on in the school.

So the question of talent spotting is as much about the school as an organization and what affordances are offered to school staff to 'be and become' leaders, as it is about what staff actually do (see Gronn and Lacey, 2004, on the importance of 'positioning space' where people can imagine themselves as heads).

The risks inherent in talent spotting are that a narrow group is recognized as being worthy of leadership development (Box 2.3). This in turn (re)produces existing (gendered and raced) norms of leadership and alienates those who have not been chosen. Failure to be 'spotted' might lead some to decisions to leave the profession altogether. It is vital that the role that the school and its existing leadership/management may have had in producing the behaviours that are seen to constitute 'talent' are not ignored.

Risky assumption 2: Potential leaders will identify themselves

Many succession planning programmes offer opportunities for teachers to volunteer for leadership/management. Teachers might, for example, approach

Box 2.3 The problem of not being spotted

I've got a member of staff who joined us in September and she's been great and she came as our Key Stage 1 leader and she had joined our leadership team, which is huge but she'd been at the same school for twenty years and been through a series of heads and suddenly realised that maybe there was more that she could do, and I know she wants to go on to deputy headship but feels that she's probably left it too late. By not having that sort of clear path in her mind and being in the right place at the right time, it's too easy to stay. I don't know how we get around training people for moving through their career and building the skills and the understanding.

(Primary head, UK)

their line manager and ask how to access leadership training, or might through some kind of performance review process identify the headship as their career goal.

Given the range of reported avenues for becoming a head outlined at the beginning of this chapter, and the varying time scales through which it happens, it is difficult to assume that there is any particular time or career stage at which people declare themselves interested in headship. It is also difficult to detach the decision to pursue leadership/management from the work and family context in which people find themselves. It is not hard to imagine teachers with demanding family responsibilities who refrain from putting themselves forward even if they are interested (Woodfield, 2007). It is also not hard to imagine a minority background teacher struggling with the possibility of being both a token representative of diversity as well as with the experience of being culturally isolated in a White majority leadership programme (McKenley and Gordon, 2002). Or someone who works for a charismatic workaholic headteacher thinking that there is no way they could possibly do the job.

The risks in relying on people to identify themselves for succession planning are that only some people will see themselves in and/or able to do the job, and thus a significant number of potential leaders will be lost to the system (Lumby, 2003). This in turn will perpetuate a particular kind of leader/manager, one who is overtly careerist and/or in an advantaged social and family situation.

Risky assumption 3: Succession programmes create a pool of school leaders

The three difficulties with this assumption are that:

1 *training and application are not the same thing*: The assumption of succession planning can be that participation in a training programme equates to a decision to apply for headship. This is not necessarily the case. A study in Missouri (Forsyth and Smith, 2002) found that only 25 per cent of those who had the appropriate licensure qualification actually took up posts. Most of that number obtained their promotion within the first 12 months of licensure. Many of the remainder chose to stay in other educational posts rather than become heads, but over 30 per cent disappeared altogether from the education system within five years of licensure. A similar finding emerged in Connecticut (Beaudin *et al.*, 2002): at the time of this research, the state had the largest number of teachers certified for headship at any time in its history but was facing increasing difficulty in filling posts.

These studies are important. They suggest that at least some teachers might take up training for headship as a general professional development opportunity and that some who take it up might be wondering whether

the headship *and/or* the profession is for them or not. The training is part
of the decision-making process, rather than its fruition.

Some English research has reported that almost all English NPQH
candidates envisage becoming a headteacher at some point in the future
(Stevens *et al.*, 2005). This may be what happens. Or it may be that
intentions do not translate into practice and what eventuates is more like
the Missouri case. Or it may be that the requirement to engage in a
mandatory leadership qualification only attracts those who already see
themselves as ready for and interested in headship. In other words, training might act as a way of preventing the groups of teachers who previously 'just fell' into leadership from doing so. Or it may simply be that
only people who were 'good products' of the NPQH answered the survey.

2   *numbers of aspirant heads does not equal posts filled*: It is possible to assume that
there are x jobs coming up and y people willing and qualified, therefore there
is no supply problem. But this happily ignores the evidence that the supply
problem occurs in particular school types and places (Chapter 1). Having
a large pool of prospective heads may simply mean more competition for
a limited number of jobs in desirable locations, and no change for schools
where it is difficult to attract a range of qualified and suitable candidates.

In addition, being trained does not in reality equate with being
experienced enough to win positions (or to do them well if they are won).
Research with serving heads almost always reports the value they place on
working with experienced heads and having the opportunity to take leadership roles and to 'act up' despite the lack of support (Bright and Ware,
2003). However, the presence of large numbers of Deputy Heads who
have no intention of moving from their position into headship places real
blockages in the path of aspirant applicants further down the school hierarchy and may well prevent them from accessing the in school experience
they need to ensure that they win positions (Hayes, 2005).

Equations between training and supply also ignore the impact that the
actual experience of applying for headship might actually have. An Australian study of Catholic school teachers (D'Arbon *et al.*, 2002, p. 475)
disaggregated the pool of potential headteachers to include: (a) 'unavailed
aspirants' who had applied for a head's position in the past and would not
do so in the future; and (b) 'unpredictables' who had applied for a position in the past but were unsure whether they would continue to do so, as
well as (c) 'potential aspirants' who had not yet applied for a position but
envisaged doing so in the future; (d) 'active aspirants' who were actively
seeking a position; and (e) 'uncertain aspirants' who would only apply for
a position if it was in a suitable location for them.

This study and others that examine teachers' attitudes to selection procedures (e.g. Blackmore *et al.*, 2006; Lacey, 2002), suggest that failure in
the application process is a big disincentive to continued application. If
there are large numbers of qualified teachers applying for a small number of

'attractive' jobs, then there is inevitably going to be a number in the 'una-vailed aspirant' category who will never apply again. While they are technically available in the pool of potential heads, in reality, they are not.

3   *targeting training is problematic*: In the Australian context, no mandatory headship qualification exists. States have largely targeted leadership training to those who already had some leadership experience in the school, since it was assumed they would want to go further – middle leaders, assistant and deputy headteachers, and/or to those in mid-career. But one study of the age profiles of Australian teachers (Preston, 2002) suggests that large numbers of middle managers and other senior administrators were in the same age band as headteachers and would retire at much the same time. In addition, the middle career group of teachers was relatively small in number *and* were people whose careers had been blocked by the baby boomer generation who occupied the bulk of leadership positions. Fur-thermore, many had also experienced long periods of temporary employment as population growth slowed and less teachers were required. However, the youngest generation of teachers who might reasonably then be expected to make up the next generation of leaders were also relatively small in number and survey data suggested that significant numbers of them did not see headship as a possibility (Lacey, 2002) or teaching as a permanent career choice (Ministerial Council of Employment Education Training and Youth Affairs, 2003). In addition, another survey suggested that men rather than women were attracted to those leadership succession programmes which required self-identification (Dorman and D'Arbon, 2003b).

In the case of Australia, then, succession plans targeted at the middle career teachers hit a somewhat jaded and insufficient number of teachers. If they include younger teachers, there is no certainty that engagement in leadership training might be enough to make them change their minds about staying in the profession. The risk is that they take their leadership/management training with them when they go. This situation has equivalents in other jurisdictions, including England.

Risky assumption 4: The way to get heads for hard-to-staff schools is to 'grow your own'

Despite the difficulties of getting applicants, some rural and inner-city loca-tions have resolved their supply question by 'growing their own' leadership through local talent-spotting and the development of local succession schemes. For grow your own schemes to be successful there must be appro-priate locally supported school-based practices (Crow and Matthews, 1998; Mullen and Cairns, 2001; Zellner *et al*., 2002), namely

- the development of a range of leadership and team-work opportunities within the school/clusters of schools;

- formal processes which allow teachers to experience a range of leadership and 'acting up' positions;
- the time for leadership 'trainees' to reflect on the practices of leadership and management both individually and with others;
- some formal input on educational and leadership theory;
- the opportunity to have formal conversations about careers, and career development processes such as 'shadowing, networking, peer-coaching, and learning walks in other schools' (Rhodes *et al.*, 2006);
- the dialogic engagement of experienced school leaders with aspirants.

There are three potential difficulties with grow your own schemes. The first is that while local initiatives might provide a ready set of applicants for positions, it may shift practice to a preference for local leaders rather than 'outsiders'. As a result, the community may not benefit from 'new blood', new ideas and different ways of doing things. The second risk is that in growing local leaders with local knowledge and local ways of doing things, less desirable practices may be reproduced along with the good. Howley and her colleagues (Howley *et al.*, 2005 p. 777), for example, warn of the dangers of developing 'old boys networks' and suggest that 'a district may want to take steps to demonstrate a commitment to social justice by nurturing a group of potential principals whose characteristics are even more diverse than its teaching staff'.

A third possibility is that problems may arise for home-grown leaders when they attempt to leave home. This was certainly the case in our Australian study where heads in country locations reported that their local experience was not seen as being sufficiently broad; they were uncompetitive in the application crush for desirable midsize middle-class city primary schools.

There are thus potential risks involved in home-grown activities – the potential for inequitable practice to evolve, for the erection of unintended barriers to incomers and for career stalling beyond the local environment.

The risk of partial solutions

The risks in assuming easy equations between succession planning schemes and supply are multiple. They may simply be another form of professional development, they might exclude the very people that are most needed in headship, they might only attract particular kinds of people, they might fail to fill positions in the schools that are most in need. However, the provision of succession planning might stimulate debate about what counts as good training for headship. This, however, is not always the case (Brundrett, 2001).

Most often, systems rely on small groups of selected heads together with 'leadership staff' for the development of succession training. They work selectively with pieces of research and their own experiences to develop training 'packages' which can be 'delivered' to aspirants in various sites. Nevertheless most attempt to achieve elements of what Houle (2006) calls 'job-embedded' professional development. He suggests that this ideal can be reduced to rhetoric unless the voices of the participants are used in a reflective process shaping the overall format and content of long-term professional development. This does happen to varying extent in succession programmes, but these are usually evaluated by a survey of participants rather than an ongoing conversation, and modified without widespread consultation. Programmes are also subject to pressures of time, money and capacity (Riley and Mulford, 2006). Furthermore, they must generally demonstrate to policy-makers that graduates are able to implement current policy agendas.

It is thus not really surprising that succession programmes are often criticized as: being too paper-based; being too focused on the individual school and not enough on the broader political multi-agency context in which schools operate; ignoring deep pedagogical learning and important debates; or not providing the resources for the complex ethical decisions heads must make (Coleman, undated; Dempster and Berry, 2003; Elmore, 2000; Smithers and Robinson, 2006). Nevertheless, despite the risks caused by poorly designed leadership training and those which arise from unexamined assumptions about effectiveness and appropriateness, the fact is that training for leadership does now exist in most countries. The NSCL in England, for example, is a hugely expensive and ambitious institution which does satisfy many who undertake its programmes (Male, 2001). A significant number of school systems have also expended significant sums on other forms of leadership development.

In reality, there has been *much* more progress in the training part of the solution to the 'supply problem' than there has been on the policy front. However, some policy options are being developed.

One policy strategy is that non-educators might take up vacant posts. The appointment of non-educators as heads is a solution which is on the English policy table, where changes to the legal capacity of governing bodies, highlighted in a commissioned report on new possibilities for school leadership (PricewaterhouseCoopers, 2007), are now equated with governing bodies using all means at their disposal to make an appointment.[2] But heads from outside the education system are unlikely to have had the opportunity to 'author' themselves as *educational* leaders (see p. 30) and thus must see themselves as generic managers who just happen to be in a school. For this reason the 'hired gun' solution is highly offensive to many in the profession and carries with it yet another set of potential risks produced from a lack of deep educational expertise at the top to underpin decision-making (Eisinger and Hula, 2004; Smithers and Robinson, 2006).

Another policy strategy is to develop new forms of headship and consultancies which offer different career opportunities for experienced heads. This holds out hope to aspirants of a more varied leadership career as well as enticing some experienced heads to stay on, rather than leave or retire. But this strategy must be seen in the light of downsized local authority and central offices, the place where sizeable numbers of heads might once have found career changes. No-one has yet done the research which examines whether federations and consultancies have created a net increase in post-headship jobs or simply reshuffled the same number of positions beyond headship of a single site. It is also far too soon to ascertain whether this is an effective supply solution. Given the attendant risks attached to headship *per se* (a focus that is coming up), it is not obvious, for example, that moving to an executive headship position will at best be more than a very partial solution to the 'supply problem'.

The most glaring gap in the supply problem-policy solution still lies in the comparative absence of strategies to address headteachers' workload, the nature of the work and its impact on personal and family life. Sidelining this set of issues in the supply problematization is to ignore the evidence from numerous surveys of teacher and headteacher attitudes to school leadership. Teachers report over and over again that what they see in and as the job of headteacher *does* affect their decision about whether to apply or not.

If doing nothing about succession planning is a risk, and if succession planning itself contains numerous risks, then the risk involved in ignoring what actually happens in the headteacher's everyday work is at least as great. Getting people ready to apply for a job is no solution at all if they are still put off by what they perceive as the reality. Training is a partial solution, policy must be comprehensively attended to as well.

The remainder of the book explores what else might be done to address the 'supply problem'. After succession planning, then what?

Part II

Rethinking the supply problem

Part II examines aspects of headship that are often out of focus in supply problem conversations. It explores what it is that we ask of headteachers, and considers how this might affect decision-making about headship. Chapter 3 proposes three 'pictures' of school leadership. Two are clearly fictions. The third, job advertisements for headteacher vacancies, claims to represent reality. It then goes on to consider the time it takes heads to meet these expectations. I compare what is routinely asked of heads in managing predictable issues related to staffing, buildings and families. I also look at the unexpected crises which can push schools and their heads to breaking point and the systems of audit which can punish heads for failing to live up to expectations and demands.

The argument in this part is that failing to take these aspects of the job seriously runs the dual risks of: (1) failing to persuade many teachers to change their mind about the desirability of headship, and (2) failing to address what causes some heads to leave their posts prematurely.

Chapter 3

Head of the pack

The problem of great expectations

In the phenomenally successful *Harry Potter* children's books, J.K. Rowling invented a headteacher now beloved by children everywhere. He is clearly a fiction, but also one representation of an ideal school leader. The head of *Hogwarts School of Witchcraft and Wizardry,* a school whose mission is to educate the future generation of witches and wizards to become productive members of a good society, is Professor Dumbledore. Rowling presents Dumbledore as appropriately venerable, possessed of the flowing gown, white beard and hair associated with all representations of wise and good wizards – Merlin, Gandalf and the like. His title, Professor, immediately signals that this is a knowledgeable head. We deduce that Dumbledore rose through the teaching ranks and we are told that his career progression was achieved through the practical demonstration of exceptional skills and learning. In other words, Dumbledore knew a lot about what his students needed to learn, and was thus genuinely a head*teacher*.

Dumbledore's task was to run his boarding school well, ensuring that novice magicians learned, through the curriculum and the lived experience of the school community, how life in the wider world should be. As a member of the International Confederation of Wizards and Chief Warlock of the Wizengamot, he also had a professional leadership brief outside of the school (now known as system leadership, see Hopkins and Higham, 2007). Dumbledore was an ethical head (Starratt, 2003; Strike *et al.,* 1998) both in the school and in the wider world. He modelled what was right, sat Solomon-like in judgement on disciplinary misdemeanours, and took a lead in defeating the forces of darkness by protecting, advocating for, and supporting the battles of a vulnerable student from an unhappy home, Harry Potter.

Professor Dumbledore did have some tricks not generally available to the average headteacher. He possessed a magic wand. There can be very few practising headteachers who have not at some stage wished for such a device to make some things/people/events vanish and to accomplish tedious tasks instantly. It is an enormously appealing fantasy to think that the unending stream of faxes, emails, forms, memos and policy documents that are the lot of today's school heads (Blackmore, 1999; Day *et al.*, 2000) might be dealt with by a simple wave of a wand.

But a wand and an extensive knowledge of White Magic were not all that equipped Dumbledore for his job as head. He had an infallible, talking, magic hat which sorted students into their appropriate 'houses' at the commencement of their enrolment in the school. This was much quicker and more effective than the laborious and often contentious task of dealing with the enrolment forms, transferred student files and parent complaints most heads face. Dumbledore also had a colourful Phoenix, which swooped in to help young Harry in times of distress. In between times it did the occasional bit of message carrying. Among his other tools of trade were a pensieve, a receptacle for his thoughts and memories, a fireplace through which he and others could travel and a collection of objects which alerted him to the presence of evil. The computer and CCTV camera are perhaps the nearest analogous equivalents for today's school administrators.

Dumbledore's moral principles supported the fair treatment of all, regardless of their birth or past. Dumbledore believed that most people were redeemable and would rise to the occasion if they were entrusted with responsibility. He positively embraced difference: appointments to Hogwarts' staff included teachers of mixed species and some with chequered pasts, werewolves and ex-prisoners. Dumbledore's professional code of ethics meant that children and adults both deserved and got second and third chances. Students and Hogwarts' staff had high expectations of him which were always fulfilled, if not immediately and in the ways that were immediately obvious.

In Dumbledore, then, readers are presented with an uncomplicated and romantic representation of a particular kind of moral headship – one in which ethical practice does not stop at the school gate, but works more widely for the greater good and in the interests of justice. Yet readers also encounter Dumbledore as a somewhat aloof figure, distanced from the staff and students, often alone in his office from which he magically appeared when needed. This distantiation does not speak of a leader who is democratic and keen to dismantle hierarchy: to the contrary it points to the ways in which he and his power were shut away from the everyday activities of the school. The presence of Prefects and Houses locked in competitions for points also highlights a school which is organized on traditional lines. Hogwarts had a clear chain of command rather than being a democratic learning community.

And Dumbledore *is* rather like the ideal espoused in treatises on the great public school heads:

> [W]e shall easily recognize the Ideal and Perfect Headmaster (*sic*) when he comes because, in one man, he will be a triple colossus: excellent as a scholar, impeccable as an organizer, inspiring as a leader. Apart from that he will have about him a tang of aloof authority well able to exercise firm rule yet showing friendliness and compassion. He will keep abreast

of the educational times yet be so sensitive to tradition that he will hand on undiminished the heritage of the ages. He will find time to promote the good name of his school as well as all the good works within it. In spite of all this, he will manage to remain human, acceptable to his friends and tolerable to his family. Naturally to do all of this he will need to have the constitution of a carthorse, the nerves of a gladiator and the resilience of a sorbo ball. Such is the ideal of the perfect headmaster which we have at the back of our minds, such is the ideal towards which we lurch.

(Goodwin, 1968, p. 13)

Dumbledore was a far cry from a modern, more business-like head.

A thoroughly modern manager

The leadership/management of Dumbledore is contrasted with that of Dolores Umbridge who, in the fifth book in the *Harry Potter* series, arrives at Hogwarts as a Ministry-appointed teacher.

The toad-like Umbridge used a lexicon and mode of thought that resonates strongly with those used by many contemporary politicians and educational bureaucracies (Fairclough, 2000). On her very first evening at Hogwarts, she interrupted Dumbledore's introductory welcome to students to make a speech about a new era of openness, effectiveness and accountability. Umbridge had a thorough knowledge of current education policy. In her initial Defence against the Dark Arts class, she told students that they would be following a carefully structured, theory-centred Ministry-approved course: this meant reading a text book on which they were to be regularly tested. Before long, the Ministry of Magic had appointed Umbridge as a High Inquisitor. She had the requisite accountability skills in school self-evaluation and school management, and her task was to assist 'school improvement' by inspecting all of the teaching staff – and ensuring that Dumbeldore's influence was curtailed.

Umbridge set herself up as a rival to Dumbledore. Her authority was obtained from the government and exercised bureaucratically. She made life miserable for the staff loyal to Dumbledore and ignored the moral code he espoused and to which the vast majority of staff were committed. The power she had was translated into a plethora of petty, officious decrees, the prescription of new rules and the application of partial punishments which allowed some sycophantic students to unfairly accumulate privileges. She outlawed student clubs, observed lessons with a checklist and a bitter smile, read students' mail, ensured that many long-serving teachers were put on probation, gave the power to inflict physical punishment to the unpleasant but formerly harmless caretaker and established a cadre of student leaders, a student 'secret police', whose powers to punish were equal to Prefects.

Dumbledore did not remain passive in the face of Umbridge's violation of his principles. Illustrating Sergiovanni's (1992) principle of 'outrage' at injustice, even if it means resistance or outright refusal to do what is expected, the venerable wizard directly opposed the increasingly nasty bureaucrat when she manoeuvred the sacking of a teacher for alleged incompetence. Dumbledore's moral code put the welfare of those who do no harm over organizational allegiance to those bent on malice and self-promotion. For a short time, he was replaced as Head by the noxious Umbridge, until the inevitable showdown provided the climax via which Dumbledore was restored to the headship of Hogwarts.

In the Dumbelore and Umbridge contest lurks a familiar present-day construct – leadership good, management/managerialism bad. The leadership mantra is one which dominates contemporary school systems and their training provisions. However, heads are not only expected to lead but also to 'deliver', that is also manage, government policy. In fact, today's headteachers must meet a range of leadership *and* management expectations – their own, that of parents and students and that of their employer. Some of those expectations are embedded in job advertisements, as are shades of both Dumbledore, and Umbridge.

Expectations, expectations, expectations

When school governing bodies or districts advertise for positions they must make a conscious decision about what to put in their advertisement. Attracting the right candidates and ultimately the right head means both selling the school and specifying must-haves: if applicants do not have some specific attributes/ qualities/skills, then the school won't be interested. Advertisements can be taken as *one*, but not the only representation, of what is expected of headteachers.

I took the 18th January 2008 issue of the *Times Educational Supplement*, a random date, and examined all the advertisements for headteachers. There were 185 in total, with 40 secondary schools, 5 sixth form colleges, 5 nurseries, and 135 primary and infant schools. 36 were faith schools, 31 of these were primary and 5 were secondary. I asked first, what the personal characteristics were that were named in the advertisements and, second, what the head was actually to do. I worked only with what was stated in advertisements. I did not work from the named practices to infer what skills, knowledge or dispositions the head might need: I assumed that what was stated was what was considered most important. While this content analysis[1] speaks to the specifics of the English school system, the general points are more widely applicable.

All there in black and white: advertised vacancies and expectations

My analysis showed that:

1 *schools were relatively vague about the headship experience required.* Only 72 of the advertisements specified senior management experience and/or proven

track records in leadership and management at senior levels. Sixth form colleges in particular all cited the number of staff and the size of the budget as a clear indicator of the level of skills and experience they were looking for. While it could be implied that this was what most were hoping for, only one specified that applicants had to have already been a headteacher. Five said that their post would be ideal for someone looking for a new challenge. The schools had all, bar one, left a way open for deputies, assistants and advisers to apply and to make a case for fitting the criteria. One noted that it wasn't experience that mattered but 'what you bring'.

2 *schools were very clear that they wanted a head who would help them change a little.* The vast majority of schools wanted a head who would take them from where they were to the next stage of development. In the majority of cases this was specified in OfSTED terms – from satisfactory with some good qualities to good, or from good to outstanding, or from outstanding onwards. In only a handful of cases was there any intimation that the school wanted an entirely new direction, a radical rethink, a new broom. This is hardly surprising since these advertisements would have to have been approved by governors who, by definition, have a stake in the ways the school currently operates and the directions it is to take.

3 *schools wanted a head who would help them to be measurably 'improved'.* Most schools wanted to improve 'standards'. Only 18 schools specified that the new head must work for something other than test results and/or man-dated outcomes specified in school self-evaluations (e.g. an imaginative curriculum; recognize the balance of academic and social; innovative and relevant curriculum; academic, social, spiritual, emotional well-being) while a further seven referred to children reaching their full potential, which could be read as something more than the formal mandated curriculum, and a further six referred to extracurricular activities (e.g. sport, art and music being 'what children want'). In addition, one secondary school asked for leadership in pedagogy and six spoke of learning, three nurseries and infant schools referred to early years practice, and 24 primary schools explicitly mentioned learning/teaching/curriculum/education, including two who wanted someone who would work on life-long learning. It might possibly be inferred here that pedagogical and curriculum expertise is now at deputy or assistant head level, or that it is implied in the notion of standards. However the majority of advertisements were not looking for a head who was highly knowledgeable about curriculum, pedagogy and assessment and who would focus on educational leadership. Rather, they highlighted the more Umbridge-like task of dealing with Ministry-required standards.

4 *schools required some kind of articulated moral basis for leadership.* Perhaps to counterbalance this, while only two schools specified integrity, the majority all included some statement which conveyed some kind of ethics. For faith schools, this was a requirement to be of a particular religion, or at

least support, a Christian/Catholic/Anglican ethos and education. For the remainder it was a more inchoate set of statements about the well-being of all children; in specific locations it was recognizing, valuing and working with ethnic and cultural diversity. The majority of schools then required some Dumbledore with their Umbridge, with the possible exception of one school which stated a preference for someone with pragmatic leadership.

5 *schools valued charisma over collaboration*. The advertisements also specified a profoundly twenty-first-century set of personal qualities:

- 68 schools required a head with vision and 9 someone visionary. 11 wanted someone to deliver a vision. Only 7 invited candidates to share a vision, and a further 2 to 'join our vision'.
- 55 wanted someone inspirational and a further 56 wanted someone who would inspire/motivate/challenge/enthuse staff, students, parents, governors, various partners; 7 wanted someone that would make the school a source of inspiration for others.
- Only 15 were explicit about a requirement for the head to be collaborative or to be part of a team, lead a team or join a team. A handful referred to themselves as a happy school which the candidate would be joining and maintaining.

Here we have a hint of the ways in which the head is different from other staff. She/he has narrative prowess. She/he is expected to develop a dream for the school and then get others to accept it. She/he has the power to get people out of their comfort zone and working hard. Because of this she/he must take responsibility for the actions of other people in the school community. She/he is not expected to operate democratically and be the convenor of a group dreaming, but is rather more like a CEO exhorting staff at a sales convention, or a general urging troops into battle.

6 *schools specified particular personal qualities*. The advertisements intimated the kinds and amount of emotional labour required of heads.

- 65 wanted someone with enthusiasm and energy and 23 wanted someone who was creative, innovative, imaginative and/or entrepreneurial. 30 wanted someone with drive, and who was dynamic, and a further 19 wanted someone who was passionate about improvement/standards/ learning/multiculturalism.
- 41 wanted someone committed or dedicated, while a further 41 wanted someone committed to standards/improvement/self-evaluation (less often children's education, Every Child Matters, early years practice). Some 29 wanted someone strong.
- there were interesting minority requirements: strategic (3); reflective (1); adaptable (1); flexible (1); versatile (1), having judgement (1).

These, then, were to be heads who were continually on the go, always 'up', brimming with new ideas and with the know-how and connections to bring them to fruition. They were not to be wishy-washy, indecisive or hesitant, but always confident and assured of what they and the school did. And in doing this, they must, as seen before, take everyone with them.

7 *schools required someone good at connecting with people.* Schools expected that heads would be active outside the school. Some 46 schools wanted someone who could build partnerships with the school community and stakeholders. In faith schools, this specifically included parishes and in some cases the archdiocese. These new heads were expected to act both within and without the school in continuous high-energy mode. Thus, it is hardly surprising that 63 were keen to get someone with good interpersonal and communication skills and 40 were determined to get someone outstanding, exceptional, gifted or talented – rather than the 13 who just wanted someone suitably qualified. But only 20 primary schools wanted someone who was caring, empathetic, had compassion, was sensitive in the ways they dealt with children and issues, or who was approachable. A further 18 schools specified a sense of humour, fun and enjoyment.

8 *schools embodied a highly gendered version of leadership.* These job advertisements articulate a relatively hard-nosed, masculinist, performative version of leadership (cf. Blackmore, 1999; Blackmore and Sachs, 2007). They have a marked preference for qualities associated with a stereotypical and narrow version of masculinity which many women and some men might find problematic. The qualities asked for are rational rather than also emotional, calculating rather than also intuitive, planned rather than also spontaneous, directive rather than cooperative, self-protecting and defended rather than also vulnerable and open, single-minded and tireless rather than balancing work and home. A few primary schools had clearly consulted children about their requirements and these were the ones which included more stereotypically 'feminine' behaviours such as care. Of course it may well have been the case that after the advertisements, and in the actual job selection processes, some more 'feminine' qualities hiding behind the baldness of 'good interpersonal and communication skills' were those which counted significantly. However, the limited research undertaken on job interviews suggests that this may well not be the case, and that it is the rational and hardnosed which also counts in interview (Blackmore *et al.*, 2006; Brooking, 2004).

9 *schools were probably wildly over-optimistic.* While statements apparently from children included 'being good at assemblies', 'being a good storyteller', 'being proud of our school', one – perhaps a reference to Dumbledore and his magic wand and hat – 'making our dreams come true', seems to sum up the overall effect of these advertisements. One has to wonder, when '2,600 schools advertised for a new head teacher for the first time during 2007' (Howson, 2008, p. 2) whether there are simply that many extraordinary, visionary, exemplary potential heads out there who can take their school from failing to outstanding, raise test results and make

partnerships with all and sundry in the community, while at the same time enthusing the staff, students and parents. One school did disarmingly offer to provide halo polish, which they then suggested the head might need to use every day!

The question raised by this analysis is whether job advertisements should focus on the ideal headteacher, or whether they should be more realistic about what is actually achievable.

You can't always get what you want

Maybe in times and places where policy is not so firmly directed towards quantifiable learning outcomes, then more mention might be made of the softer side of school leadership. When the outcomes of schooling are not so firmly steered towards the achievement of test scores, and a style of leadership which must engage in very particular kinds of performance management, knowledge about pedagogy and curriculum, for example, might be valued more highly. It would be interesting to compare these advertisements with those from a different time and/or place. While I did not do this, I did find research which had.

Patrick Whitaker (1983), writing before the UK Education Act of 1988 changed the scope and scale of responsibilities of English schools through what is generally known as 'devolution' or 'site-based management', addressed the issue of primary headteacher advertisements and what they said about the role. At this time headteachers were still employed by the local authority and not the school governing body as was the case post-1988. Advertisements were placed in the local press, and Whitaker cites three which he says are 'fairly typical':

> Required for January a headteacher with experience of modern teaching methods and working among children from multi-ethnic backgrounds and with an awareness of community links.
>
> Headteachers required. Appointment to take effect as soon as possible. This is an interesting and challenging post for an enthusiastic person. Application forms and further particulars ...
>
> The vacancy arises from the promotion of the previous holder of the post and it is hoped that the successful candidate will take up duty as from April, or earlier possible. The post offers admirable scope for a teacher of energy and initiative.
>
> (ibid., pp. 9–10)

The contrast with the 2008 expectations is striking. Perhaps local authority expectations were then too low, or maybe they were simply less utopian than today's English governing bodies. However, Whitaker goes on to say

'Enthusiasm and energy seem to be the qualities that most LEAs prize, although it sometimes appears that availability is the strongest qualification of all' (ibid., p. 10).

The continuity of the physical–emotional description of headship is significant and is testament that the job of school leadership has *always* been one which is challenging and which places specific kinds of demands on the person filling the role. This can also be seen in an advice book for new heads from the late 1960s which began: 'All Heads possess certain qualities in common: integrity of character, mental vigour, immense reserves of emotional energy, physical stamina, sound judgment, the ability to make decisions yet the will to consult and involve others in the process' (Edmonds, 1968, p. vii). The reasons for heads to have energy and stamina lie deep in the heart of everyday leadership/management practice. Harry Wolcott's (1973) ethnographic study of a year in the life of one elementary school head was the first to document the typical headteachers' daily mix of formal and informal encounters and routines, the constant anticipation and resolution of problems and the inevitable passing of judgement on a myriad of matters, all of which could have serious consequences if got wrong. There was little time to pause in between what was a constant kaleidoscope of tasks 'brought to him (*sic*) or created for him by others rather than by any grand design of his own of what he wished to accomplish' (ibid., p. 34). The press for responsiveness and the continual shifting of gears to move from one thing to another do require physical stamina, focus, concentration and the capacity to remain on an emotional even keel (see more on this in Chapter 4).

In the early 1980s, Whitaker was not contesting this. He was concerned that local authorities took the process of selection too lightly. He argued that relying on enthusiasm and experience was insufficient and that more 'honest' details about the school should be provided to candidates in advertisements. These should be much more specific about expectations. Whitaker was particularly concerned that potential heads should know the situation of the school to which they were applying. He offered 12 basic types of schools which required different attributes and practices from their headteachers: these ranged through new school, reorganized school, extended school, reducing school, star school, steady school, to confused school, unhappy school, at risk school (Whitaker, 1983, p. 7). Whitaker argued that getting the right person for the job depended on details of specific issues within the particular school being made available at the outset, because the job of headteacher selection is one of 'matching the qualities and aptitudes of the candidate to the specific requirements of the school' (ibid., p. 6).

If the cap 'fits': matching applicant and post

The contemporary set of advertisements I studied did provide some specific details about numbers on roll, but they were remarkably generic in their requirements, rather than specific about what was needed. There were two remote schools in the corpus of advertisements and they, like a handful of schools in specific 'lifestyle' locations, were candid about the particular challenges and benefits that their location provided. But only one stated that it was in special measures, another that it was on an OfSTED 'notice to improve' and a further four noted amalgamations of two institutions. My own knowledge of the schools suggests that a significantly higher number were in an OfSTED category but this was signalled in their advertisements more by the omission of positive OfSTED comments than through admission. There was no school in this set which acknowledged any other kinds of problems or specificities.

In the bulk of advertisements I analysed a relatively homogenous kind of leader was required for what appeared to be a relatively similar group of schools. A kind of 'We'll have what they're having' seemed to be at work. Lists of 'what we offer' focused on relatively common things. Attempts to 'sell the school' were remarkably alike – happy children, calm atmosphere (less time on discipline), supportive parents, dedicated staff (less time sorting out conflicts, no problems with poor performance).

It is not likely that this uniformity actually assures applicants that all these schools are the same. Rather some intensive 'decoding' may well go on. For example, does 'must enthuse staff' actually mean 'we have a group of teachers who need a kick in the rear'? Does 'visionary' mean 'we've lost our way and we need someone to sort us out quickly'? Does 'energetic' mean ' we want you here all hours of the day and night'? Lack of specificity and homogeneity may well breed cynical interpretations.

There is no doubt that prospective heads do pick and choose, and that they are looking for different things. Not all of them are put off by 'schools in challenging circumstances', for example. What they need from an advertisement is enough information to see whether they 'match' the needs of the school.

This quest for 'fit' is not well served by the advertisements I analysed. Managing the risk of putting people off applying by euphemizing the actual circumstances of schools may, in reality, risk putting off the very applicants who are best suited to the position (see Box 3.1).

Just as Whitaker noted over two decades ago, it is of critical importance for schools to get heads who 'fit'. If a head arrives at a new post where they have one set of expectations and the governing body and school community another, there is a recipe for potential conflict and/or disappointment and/or at the very least compromise and adjustment on both sides. Box 3.2 is an illustration of contrasting headteacher expectations of the job and the consequences. If the fit between the candidate and the school is right then at the very least things get off to a good start.

The newly appointed secondary head in Box 3.1 did a lot of homework in order to find the school that was right for her. She did not simply rely on a

Box 3.1 Heads choose which schools they 'fit'

I remember when I was interviewed for a deputy's job, there were two advertised: one was (a deprived school in a regional town) and the other was in a small, comfortable country town. They wrote and said, 'Look you can have your choice, which one do you want?' and they expected me to say the small, nice country town and I said, 'I'm going to the other one'. I remember the superintendent saying, 'Why would you want to do that?' And the reason is, that's a school with character and difference, right ... I reckon it's your headset about the energy and excitement that comes in some of the schools and I guess if you went to a school where it wasn't there, on the surface, you'd have to dig down and find it. Because if you do that, then you do develop the focus on educational leadership and purpose and making a difference. And that's not being rude but I think there are some schools that probably need some spark.
(Experienced secondary head, Australia)

[T]he thing that I would say about this particular job is that it was the right sort of school at the right time. I looked at other jobs and I applied for other jobs and I went for other interviews but none of them were right and I think you need that match. If you get that right, then it's really a recipe for success; you get that wrong, and it's an absolute recipe for disaster.

In fact – and it's strange for me to say this, and I think that if any other headteacher heard me they would think 'don't be so ridiculous' – but it's actually slightly easier than I thought it would be. And that might just be fortunate in that I've got the right school that is right for me and I've got there at a time when they were ready for change. I don't think they quite knew what changes were required but I think they knew that they needed to change and they were in a position where they'd just gone into a category and, I think, it was kind of if you can get us out of it, we will come with you ... And I suppose it was easier having that lever which then enabled me to say that we needed to do this, this and this. I didn't know necessarily that it would work. I kept my fingers crossed and fortunately it did work and that has helped to galvanize things further so that people think that I do know what I'm talking about. And we have made quite a lot of changes and things, at the moment, have worked. I'm not saying that they will continue to work but there is nothing like having a bit of success for people to think: right, I'll get on board with it because she seems to be going in the right direction and things seem to be working. So it's a really nice position to be in and I'm sure there are other heads who would say, 'Oh, my God, it's been a nightmare. I can't believe ...' ... it is hard. I'm not saying that it's not hard; it is hard and it wears you down and it's tiring and it's stressful and you have to be somebody who can deal with that and doesn't get overwhelmed with that. And some days I come home and think, 'I'm glad the day's over'. But mainly I get up in the morning and I feel great and I feel really positive and I'm just waiting to see what the day is going to bring. I think some of it is fortune and some of it is what you do and how you do it and when the two things come together it sort of creates a situation where it is a pleasure and it is something that you look forward to and something that you feel is manageable and doable.

(New secondary head, UK)

Box 3.2 Fit for the post

[W]hen we are looking at how do we retain people in the future; how do we get the best people to take these jobs ... They have no idea of what they are going into because it's never the job that you think it will be and all the training in the world will not prepare anyone for taking on a school like this ... or even a school at the opposite end of the scale where the pressures for success are huge and actually they are as exacting as they are for us here. And that's why I just don't understand why there hasn't been a bigger national understanding or a body of work about why aren't we matching people with the right qualities and the right interpersonal skills to the jobs where they are going to need it most – because that's what's burning people out. They are being burnt out by having to put so much into some aspects of their work that they are not comfortable with. That's how I see it really. If we talk about it on a personal basis: what is it that is stopping me from wanting to carry on with this job? It's inappropriate external pressures; it's the amount of emotional effort that I have to put in and which I expect everyone else to put into the job as well. So if it's wearing for me, then it's wearing for every member of staff in our school because I model what I expect from everybody else.

(Experienced primary head, on the point of resignation, UK)

bland and uninformative job advertisement but actively sought out a school which was 'fertile ground' for the kinds of things she wanted to do. Such grapevine research relies on using informal channels to search out what is expected in a post. However, such channels of information are notoriously inaccurate and may well put good applicants off. Much safer to have the kind of information applicants need in the public domain, beginning with the advertisement. However, as the primary head in Box 3.2 suggests, if first impressions and encounters are not what is actually required day to day, year on year, then one consequence may be that the head decides to leave. There is also a significant problem in the making if both the new head and the governing body have a view that the role of headship *is* what is stated in advertisements – but this is not the reality.

In the concluding section of the chapter I return to the issue of leadership and management. I consider the kind of leadership that is promoted in these kinds of job advertisements and whether it is attractive or off-putting to prospective heads.

Blinded by the light: charismatic leadership

Dumbledore was a charismatic leader. According to *Dictionary.com*, the definition of charisma is:

- a rare personal quality attributed to leaders who arouse fervent popular devotion and enthusiasm;
- personal magnetism or charm.

Charisma was originally associated with the influence of the Christian Church and its assumption of legitimate authority on the basis of claims of privileged access to, and interpretations of, truth. As Bauman and May put it:

> We can speak of charisma whenever the acceptance of certain values is motivated by the belief that the preacher of those values is endowed with privileged powers and these guarantee the truth of their visions and the propriety of their choice.
>
> (Bauman and May, 2001, p. 66)

In times of increasing risk and uncertainty, in which former authorities are proved to be vulnerable and fallible, the charisma of the Church is now waning. Ordinary people now take as charismatic leaders the occasional politician (although politics is, like the Church, largely a disenchanted arena), self-help gurus, New Age prophets, sports personalities and television celebrities. These are the people who step in to provide solutions to shifting problems and who now have the right to determine not only what is right and wrong, but also what is the right thing to do.

There is debate about how charisma is exercised as and through leadership. But when put to the task of guiding, directing, controlling, being first, commanding and/or starting – the dictionary definitions of leading – charismatic leadership begins with a forceful, alluring, bewitching, dazzling or magnetic persona (see *Thesaurus.com*). In his weighty investigation of 'great leaders', the psychologist Howard Gardner (1996) proposed that leadership is a process of telling stories that influence others either directly or indirectly through the ideas that their stories develop. He suggested that charismatic leaders have both 'internal' narrative capacities and 'external' cultural opportunities to make their stories resonate with large numbers of people. According to other advocates, charismatic leaders have five characteristics: vision and articulation, sensitivity to the environment/context, sensitivity to organizational members and preparedness to take risks and be unconventional in their behaviour (Conger and Kanungo, 1998). These characteristics are used to sway potential followers to their point of view: followers buy the 'vision', they follow the leader. In organizations, charisma is used to enthuse, motivate, challenge, bring staff together, and deliver a vision.

The connections between this view of leadership and the job advertisements is obvious. The majority of schools asked not only for someone who had boundless energy and enthusiasm (the ongoing everyday necessity of headship) but also someone who was charismatic/transformational. They wanted someone who had a vision and would inspire others to take it up. Most schools in fact wanted a much more contemporary version of Dumbledore, an inspirational leader with magical capacities to see the future and to make it happen, someone to protect them from falling from OfSTED grace, someone to take them safely into the wicked world.

A vast tranche of leadership literature suggests that this kind of singular hierarchical leadership is inappropriate and does not produce lasting change. Instead leadership which is distributed, shared and/or democratic is advocated (Ainscow and West, 2006; Frost and Harris, 2003; Lambert et al., 1995; Spillane, 2006). Yet here in a set of 2008 job advertisements charisma is alive and well. It seems that any celebration about the demise of charismatic leadership is somewhat premature.

There is also a dark side to charisma. Sometimes charismatic leaders are motivated more by ego than altruistic motives. Their ideas are often more convincing in person when listeners are 'spellbound' by their oratory, than they are later on reflection. Charismatic leaders do not necessarily want to change anything. They often have a negative impact on their immediate followers and more broadly. Furthermore, charismatic leaders sometimes stay in any situation only long enough to mobilize team efforts, take all the credit and then leave others with the problems of putting their ideas into practice. They may well thus only have a very temporary effect and leave behind 'followers' with profound feelings of betrayal and cynicism. It is also the case that exceptional leaders of this type, and there are some in the school system, are regarded as 'hard acts to follow'. As heads, charismatic leaders may in fact put off potential replacements.

The problems with the notion of charisma have caused many to reject it and to adopt instead the notion of transformational leadership which does have a positive orientation to change (Hallinger, 1992). Transformational leadership, while different from charismatic, does, however, share with it the notion of enthusing, motivating, challenging, bringing staff together, to deliver a vision for particular ends.

Regardless of semantic niceties, images of both transformational and charismatic leadership underpin the advertised image of the 'hero head' who arrives in a puff of smoke through the selection and appointment chimney, magic wand and spells at the ready.

Charisma and management

At the same time that the job advertisements sought Dumbledore-like motivational, outstanding, exceptional, dynamic, innovative and creative leaders with vision, they also wanted aspects of Umbridge, the head who would ensure that the school ran according to Ministry requirements, implemented policy and raised standards determined elsewhere. They wanted a good manager, a decent bureaucrat.

Max Weber is the political theorist associated with developing understandings about the growth, purposes, strengths and limitations of bureaucracies. He contrasted the kinds of serendipitous organizational practices associated with charisma with those associated with bureaucracy, a rational and stable structure with predictable relationships, processes and rules. Both, he argued, were systems of domination of individuals. But the partiality and unpredictability of charisma were trumped by the application of scientific rationality. The strength of bureaucracy was in its routines and its capacity to handle demands with relative neutrality and even-handedness. As a consequence:

> the individual bureaucrat cannot squirm out of the apparatus in which he (*sic*) is harnessed … In the great majority of cases, he is only a single cog in an ever-moving mechanism which prescribes to him an essentially fixed route or march.
>
> (Weber, 1947, p. 228)

According to Weber, bureaucracy sits uneasily with charisma. Indeed, he suggests that it is almost impossible for charismatic leadership to operate untrammelled within a bureaucratic organization because 'discipline tames charisma and everything becomes more rational' (ibid., p. 261). As Samier (2002, p. 38) succinctly words it, 'the more bureaucratized social relations in an organization become, the less room there is for charisma to play a role'.

This insight raises important questions. How is it actually possible for school leaders to develop a vision for education in situations where much of what they do is prescribed and delimited, and where there can be harsh consequences for going against policy, or simply failing to live up to it? What kinds of tensions are created when mandated requirements force heads to focus on bureaucratic tasks rather than on those which are visionary? We hear a hint of some answers to these questions in the words of the heads in Boxes 3.2 and 3.3, and there will be much more in chapters to come.

For now, it is sufficient to note that job advertisements not only take up a somewhat debatable notion of charismatic leadership but they also suture

> **Box 3.3 A head's reflections on the demise of vision**
>
> [T]he accountability model is now quite clear. If you cannot deliver what the government wants for your school, you and your school will not survive. The opportunities for individual and unique expression of vision may still be available to the highest-performing school which, having everything else in place, may still have the opportunity to be visionary in methodology, but for many schools delivering higher standards is what it is about.
>
> (Cain, 1999, p. 104)

this together with bureaucratic organizational and policy demands as if there were no possible problems, no contradictions or tensions. The schools in the advertisements I examined wanted a compliant Dumbledore without curriculum and pedagogy expertise *and* an inspirational Umbridge with vitality, charm and praiseworthy ethics.

Headteachers, however, are mere mortals, not super-humans, and it may be neither realistic nor humane to ask them to live such a difficult combination.

Great expectations and the supply problem

Governors and parents all want the best headteacher they can possibly get. We can only wonder whether perfectly competent and acceptable teachers or deputy/assistant heads look at the high expectations that are embodied in job advertisements and decide that they just couldn't do what is asked. We can only speculate whether it is significant that *no* school suggested that they wanted a headteacher who could maintain a healthy balance between work and home. We can ponder who is more likely to apply to a school which asks for 'someone we can like and respect' or to one which asks for someone inspirational who will motivate and enthuse staff. It would take specific research to ascertain whether the utopian lists of requirements found in the advertisements analysed in this chapter put off any potential applicants.

The National College for School Leadership in England conducted precisely this exercise.[2] In an action research project into redesigning headship, they found that prospective heads *were* put off by advertisements which were elaborations of the national standards for headship; these put together Dumbledore and Umbridge qualities in the same ways as the job advertisements I analysed. By contrast, and in keeping with the recommendations of Whitaker (1983) over two decades before, the headship applicants in the NCSL project responded positively to contextualized descriptions of schools and honest statements of what the job required. If this group of aspirant heads is anything to go by, it may *well* be the case that prospective applicants read the vast majority of aspirational job advertisements and think that to make an application runs too many risks. They may simply fail to measure up, or if successful, may end up either seriously overworked or disappointing those who held out high hopes.

It is therefore quite likely that, in putting together and putting forward a representation of headship as a job which requires a heroic leader capable of holding the Dumbledore of charismatic leadership together with the Umbridge of bureaucratic conformity, the writers of headteacher advertisements may very well deter the very person who 'fits' their real needs and desires. Great expectations may well produce great disappointments for all concerned.

Chapter 4

Head work

The problem of time on tasks

There must now be very few people in the English-speaking world who do not know Principal Skinner – the harried headteacher who runs Springfield Elementary, the school attended by Bart and Lisa Simpson. Episodes of *The Simpsons* regularly feature Principal Skinner engaged in misguided and generally unsuccessful attempts to establish his authority: imposing ludicrous amounts of detention on Bart, running fire drills which go badly wrong, saving money on school dinners, trips and amenities, or attempting to foster an old-fashioned sense of school spirit in mystified students. While Principal Skinner's frequent flashbacks and references to his glory days as a Green Beret in Vietnam may be simply comical, his battle with officialdom in the form of Superintendent Chalmers produces sympathy. However, his home life – as an aging, lonely, lovelorn bachelor living with a mother who doles out his pay cheques as pocket money – makes him a pathetic and sad character. When Homer Simpson asks him about his personal circumstances, Principal Skinner's reply has resonance well beyond the stereotypes ironically exaggerated in the cartoon world of Springfield.

Homer Simpson: Are you married?
Principal Skinner: Only to the job …

Principal Skinner, like most of the parodic characterizations which feature in the long-running cartoon series, has the capacity to speak pointedly (Alberti, 2004, p. 55), in this case to those who are headteachers, or those who work with and watch what headteachers do. The representation of the head who has no life to speak of outside of work is chillingly close to what many say is the reality.

This chapter deals with headteachers' workload and the experiences of those who do it. It addresses the concerns expressed by teachers who say they do not want to apply for headteacher posts because it just takes too much time. The chapter canvasses the 'truth' in these perceptions.

A caveat on overwork

The intensification of work is a phenomenon experienced by many who remain in secure, paid employment (Burchell, 2001; Green, 2001). This situation has not gone unnoticed. Across the world, increasing attention is paid to the ways in which particular occupations are now working long hours at the cost of personal well-being, institutional morale, and sustainable organizational improvement.

Headteachers and the teaching workforce are thus not the only occupational group to voice their concerns about overwork and stress. Such expressions of concern derive from general changes in the nature and cultures of work which include:

- *changed organizational forms.* The trend in the West is for 'flatter' and less hierarchical organizations where fewer managers work longer hours and have greater autonomy and responsibility (Handy, 1995).[1] In the public sector, New Public Management (NPM) (Hood, 1995) also saw the role of the 'downsized' centre change to become that of policy development and monitoring. Service delivery and policy implementation became local responsibilities. In education, as in other areas of the public sector, the introduction of devolved NPM structures shifted changed roles, new accountabilities and workload from the centre to the periphery.
- *changed work technologies.* The development of all-day/all-night global communication systems has profoundly affected the nature and hours of many, including the finance industry, journalism, information services and higher education. In education, much headteacher work is now 'virtual' and can be taken anywhere at any time.
- *ongoing dispositions and habits.* Professional ethics steer members towards work completion. One study of the work of professional and 'blue-collar' workers (Nippert-Eng, 1996) found that professionals were much less likely to create boundaries between work and home and often allowed their work to take up significant physical and temporal space at home once they had left their actual place of work. Heads are no exception to this.
- *greedy organizations* (Coser, 1974). Contemporary devolved organizations require daily dedication and commitment rather than loyalty in perpetuity. They need employees who identify with their work/role and who will give their selves to accomplish corporate goals (Hochschild, 1997). They reward work addiction (Gini, 2001). Heads may thus be partially implicated in their own overwork.
- *changed expectations.* Over a century of industrial struggle and negotiation has created expectations that all employees have the right to expect a good and safe working environment. Heads are responsible for administering occupational health and safety legislation and are perhaps more

aware than many of the ideal of the safe workplace and the balanced lifestyle and its connections to stress, burnout and ill health.

While heads are not alone in working very hard, there are particular consequences of their situation.

Weighing up the risks

At the beginning of the book I argued that the contemporary proliferation of risks meant that all of us were continually engaged in processes of risk assessment, risk planning and risk management. This chapter works from the premise that teachers do, or do not, apply for headteacher positions because they have conducted an informal risk assessment and found the job either worth the risks – or not. Although there is some evidence about the processes involved in making decisions to apply for headship, very little of the research about the supply problem has probed the *basis* on which teachers make decisions not to apply for specific positions. Most research simply canvasses their general attitudes and intentions. While we know that teachers *are* concerned about the possible impact of headship on the rest of their everyday lives (see Chapter 1), we are not clear where this information comes from.

It is reasonable to assume that teachers have a 'vernacular' knowledge (McLaughlin, 1996) of headteachers' work which comes from being in close proximity to one or a number of headteachers. Teachers see the head's car in the car park when they arrive and when they leave at night. When they begin a new school term, they are aware that the head has already been at work for some time. They themselves feel able to contact the head before and after school, on weekends and during the holidays. They also know that the head has many after-school meetings to attend (see Box 4.1).

But this first-hand knowledge is not the only place where teachers find out about the workload involved in school leadership. Two other likely sources of

Box 4.1 Teacher reluctance

Senior English teacher Karen Del Purgatorio has been in the classroom for 10 years, and as a respected teacher she's the type of person which might be sought out to some day lead a school. Yet she watches principals and vice principals at the 3,000 Deer Valley High School in Antioch scurry from parent complaint to district meeting to evening football game, always aware that their job is on the line if they can't raise student test scores. She knows with certainty she wouldn't want their jobs.

(*San Francisco Chronicle*, 23 September 2001, www.tomorrow.org/ csnews_articles04.html (accessed 21 August 2002)

information that teachers might use in order to decide what it is that heads do are: (1) public data about workload; and (2) public discussions of the job. Here I use both to explore some key findings about both the hours and the nature of headteachers' work.

Counting the hours

We do know something about how many actual hours teachers work and this has not ignored by policy-makers. In England and Wales, for example, there have been regular union surveys of teacher workload. In response to teachers' concerns, employers have initiated policy for increased use of para-professional staff (workforce remodelling), and a plethora of advice on how to manage stress and 'work–life balance'. However, the situation is a little different for heads.

In 2007, the English National Association of Head Teachers released the results of an on-line survey (French and Daniels, 2007). Almost half the school leaders reported working between 49 and 59 hours a week during term time, with a further two-fifths reporting a 60-hour week (ibid., p. 9). While this eased up during the holiday period, the overall picture, according to the report's authors:

> [makes it] clear that school leaders have long, increasingly unsocial, working hours. This reflects their attempts to deal with the expanding number and range of duties placed upon them (notably the extension of services outside of the schoolday), increasing their working hours to match an expanding workload.
>
> (ibid., p. 12)

This grim picture is supported by other studies of headteachers' work in England (PricewaterhouseCoopers, 2007), Wales (Estyn, 2007) and Ireland (Irish Primary Principals Network, 2004). Similar figures are also seen in North America; for example, a 2005 survey of Canadian principals (Blouin, 2005) reported that only 37 per cent were happy with the impact of the job on their family life and 47 per cent were satisfied or somewhat satisfied with the hours that they worked. In Victoria, Australia, a 2003 survey (Saulwick Muller Social Research, 2004) suggested that heads were working an average of 59.6 hours a week, with a 2007 survey of schools reporting increasing workload for both teachers and heads (Australian Education Union, 2007).

Few of these types of surveys are disaggregated by school type or location and they generally rely on self-reporting. There is often no external observation to confirm what it is that people say they do. These kinds of data also generally ask for a snapshot at a particular time so there is no provision for variations in work over the year, although some, such as the NAHT study, do. Furthermore, the studies often cannot say much about those heads who are not experiencing the same level of overload. Readers, therefore, have few clues as to why some heads work a lot and some don't. Nevertheless, there is such consistency over time and across locations that it must be assumed that even if the actual numbers can be queried, the general picture of overwork is true for most heads in most places most of the time (see Box 4.2).

If/when teachers read this 'factual' data about headteachers' workload, it must reinforce the observations and experiences that they make in their school. Given that some of this information is generated by headteachers' own professional associations for the purposes of political lobbying, it is important to note that, in seeking to make conditions better for current heads, they may well be helping to put off those who might next take up the post (see Box 4.2). But of course not to publicize the hours of work is to ignore what is actually happening. This is the workload Catch-22.

Box 4.2 Media reports of workload

Oh, horrendous paperwork. I don't even think about paperwork until after 4 or 5 o'clock. I don't even think about going home until around 6 or 7 o'clock at night and sometimes I don't even go home at all. Many nights I've spent the night here – there's just so much to do.

(*PBS Online Newshour with Jim Lehrer*, 25 May 2001, www.pbs.org.newshour/ bb/education/jan-june01/principal_05–22.html; accessed 1 June 2001)

His day started with a parent conference. By 7.30 he was at the front of Wilde Lake High greeting some of the 1,477 students who attend this school in Howard County. Next on the day planner, a quick speech at the madrigal festival, a demonstration English lesson and a meeting with the English Supervisor. At 11.30 he spoke to Loyola College about the state of principals in Maryland, then headed back to school for a 3pm meeting with a parent. Staff development meeting lasted from 4.30 until 6.30 and then he returned phone calls until 8. By 8.30 he was headed home – 13½ hours after he set out.

(*Washington Post*, 29 March 2001 p. B02)

'I would reckon I would work 15 or 16 hours a day.' The list of duties is frightening: meetings with staff, parents, builders, governors, psychologists, social workers and many others, assemblies to run every day in two different schools, budgets and targets to set and manage, furniture to choose, caterers to handle, staff to hire, fire and review. Myers likens it to being the managing director of a medium size plc, only with less pay. And … the prospect of a naughty child arriving at your office any minute.

(*Saturday Guardian*, 16 June 2007, Work, p. 3)

The work – same as it ever was?

The 1970s

Harry Wolcott's 1970s ethnography *The Man in the Principal's Office* (1973) begins with a description of one day in the life of elementary school principal Ed. He arrived at school at 8.10 am. He was busy the entire day and his work consisted of a series of unrelated tasks and interactions – a constant shifting from one thing to another. He got home at 6 pm and left again an hour or so later to attend two meetings and finally returned home at 10.30. His typical day was 8 am to 5 pm followed by an evening meeting (ibid., p. 89). Much of Ed's daily work was taken up with formal meetings, an unusually high number, Wolcott noted, and 'a myriad of small problems brought to him or created for him by others' (ibid., p. 34). Wolcott concluded that Ed's work could be seen as a series of formal and informal 'encounters', of which on average half was in prearranged meetings and in deliberate but not prearranged encounters, a quarter were taken up by chance encounters or an encounter on the telephone, with the remainder being primarily or available for an encounter (alone and stationary) or going to an encounter (alone and en route).

This encounter economy and the other work that Ed had to do, like his counterparts in England, were strongly framed by external control of staffing and funding. He did, however, have some areas of autonomy. John Watts, headteacher of Countesthorpe College in Leicester, wrote in the 1970s of the six powers of headteachers (Watts, 1976, pp. 129–30). These were:

1 defining the objectives and values for the school, operating within the limits of what governors set;
2 determining curriculum, what is taught;
3 control of internal organization of curriculum – timetabling, student grouping and allocation of teachers to classes;
4 distribution of available money;
5 choosing his (*sic*) own staff (within limits set by the local authority);
6 control of the media of communication which regulates who knows what about what.

Watts argued that decision-making on all six could be shared with staff, pupils and governors, without the head losing authority or influence. While Watt's position was somewhat anomalous with his peers, the balance of local power and central authority on which his argument rested was set to change.

The 1980s–1990s

In the late 1980s, Geoff Southworth also conducted an ethnographic study, *Looking into Primary Headship* (1995), with an English primary headteacher,

Ron. He found patterns of work similar to those in Wolcott's study. Ron arrived at school around 8.30 am but left at any time from 4 pm–11 pm depending on what was required. Southworth notes that Ron 'frequently worked well into the evening. It was not unusual for him to be in school two or three evenings a week. He also put in time on the weekend. In short, Ron worked long hours' (ibid., p. 87). Like Wolcott's Ed, Ron's time was mainly concerned with face-to-face meetings, but he also spent time working with documents which Southworth suggested, were not only 'a lot for him to read and digest' (ibid., p. 89) but which also created work, since he had to share the information with staff, governors and sometimes parents and students. He was also the contact point for external agencies and organizations, and was engaged in networking inside and outside of the school. Ron was frustrated by the amount of time he needed to be physically out of the school, and worried about impact of the 'national curriculum, testing and assessment, local management of schools and open enrolments' (ibid., p. 119) which he saw as 'preoccupied with administration and accountancy' (ibid., p. 122).

Southworth documented Ron's concerns about a new style of headship in which he had

> less control of his work and the school than he was accustomed to ... by limiting his power to influence others the changes threatened his occupational identity ... which he saw as being concerned with the possession and projection of an educational vision.
>
> (ibid., p. 125)

Southworth saw Ron's response as potentially being a transition phase. Once he knew what the changes meant, he would not have to be out of the school so much or be so taken up with documents. His sense of loss and anxiety about his old way of doing things could well pass.

Ron's concerns were precipitated by important shifts in the legal and administrative framework for schooling. The introduction of reforms in the UK, begun in the late 1980s and early 1990s – with counterparts in New Zealand, Alberta (Canada), most states of Australia, and some states and school districts in the USA – brought devolved budgets and responsibility for the appointment and dismissal of staff and the upkeep and development of buildings and grounds. Heads lost the capacity to determine curriculum (cf. Watts's point 2) and had greatly expanded roles in relation to management of funds and selection of staff (cf. Watts's points 4 and 5). The specification of core curriculum outcomes accompanied by the development of standardized tests and league tables required different forms of teacher planning and record-keeping and their monitoring and management (cf. Watts's point 3). There was also a new requirement for accountability and new time-consuming forms of monitoring and evaluation. The subsequent introduction of systems of audit, inspection and risk management brought new requirements for documentation and continued maintenance of computer-based data on newly developing administrative systems.

Competition between schools for enrolments combined paradoxically with demands for greater cooperation among schools to increase the number of out-of-school meetings. Heads spent more time liaising with key community stakeholders and greater engagement in community organizations. The ongoing churn of policy initiatives brought additional funds but each also had separate accountability requirements, expectations, consultations and meetings. A concern to share expertise across the system also produced for experienced headteachers expectations that they mentor, coach, train and support those new in post.

Headteachers were (and are) not necessarily opposed to a great deal of this agenda *per se* (see Box 4.3). Prior to 1988 in England, headteachers singly and collectively were highly critical of centralized systems which failed to provide the right staff at the right time, made them reliant on the priorities of external agents for security, cleaning and maintenance services, and took teachers out of school for diffuse and often less than useful training (for a comparison with Australia, see Caldwell and Spinks, 1988, 1992; Thomson, 1994). Heads were in general pleased to take control of these kinds of everyday management functions since they believed they would be more efficient.

However, they also hoped that with this responsibility would come a new kind of educational infrastructure. While larger secondary schools and some big primary schools were able to employ business managers, to this day many still are not in this position. Heads of small primary schools in particular now add a set of accounting and business functions to their everyday work simply because they have no alternative.

For most heads, it was not any one of these new tasks in isolation but their combined effects that was difficult. Taken together, these new forms of leadership, management and accountability required heads to spend large amounts of time on administrative functions necessary for the work of teachers and students to proceed smoothly.

Box 4.3 Headteachers want autonomy

'They hold principals accountable for test scores, yet we don't have the power to hire and fire teachers', Waples said. 'A principal is required to be an instructional leader, the social worker, do administrative tasks – there are just so many things we're responsible for. But the general feeling is that we're not getting the support from central administration.'

(*Washington Post,* 25 June 2000, p. A01)

Today's work and workload

A National College for School Leadership work diary-based study (Bristow *et al.*, 2007) of 34 English headteachers undertaken some 15 years after Southworth's ethnography, shows that this group worked an average of 52.9 hours for each of two weeks. The majority worked between 40 and 65 hours, with women working slightly longer than their male counterparts (ibid., p. 51). One head spent a whopping 105.6 hours while another coasted through an easy 36.4-hour week. As in earlier studies, the NCSL heads reported 'multi-tasking': they had to respond quickly to demands ranging from picking up litter to professional development discussions (ibid., p. 52). However, these reports show a distinct pattern. Heads spent 39 per cent of their time on management (staff-related issues, budget, behavioural issues, health and safety, grounds and buildings, pupil issues, assessment and examination) and administration (travel, walking around, assemblies phone calls, emails and mail, newsletter, letters, playground and lunchtime duties, teaching and cover issues, before and after school clubs, special education issues and writing and reading references). A further 17 per cent of time was spent with external stakeholders. 17 per cent of their time was devoted to staff meetings and with administration staff, and a further 17 per cent on professional development issues including mentoring and coaching. What the NCSL calls 'strategic leadership' took up only 7 per cent of their time (ibid., p. 50).

Some workload concerns do have a distinctive local colour. Worries about litigious parents often appear in US research whereas in the UK this might feature as potential conflicts with, and time demands made by, governing bodies. Boris-Schacter and Langer (2006) highlight the troublesome work produced for US headteachers through conflicts arising from differences in expectations between parents and school staff, from parent demands about special education provision, and from community responses to tests and league tables. Studies of US school reform highlight the difficulties that headteachers have to manage if they try to introduce changes which challenge established gender and race relations and/or if they attempt to shift the privilege afforded to particular groups of children and their families through tracking and setting practices (e.g. Lipman, 1998; Tittle, 1995).

The NCSL study canvassed what heads thought made the job so time-consuming. 41 per cent of the NCSL cohort nominated accountability, bureaucracy and external demands as the things that they would most like to change, with one head quoted as saying:

> Sometimes I feel that the whole system is geared up to finding the 5–10 per cent of schools who are not doing the job. The other 90 per cent have somehow got to put up with a huge amount of bureaucracy and

interference and inspection … If we could get the balance of responsibility and power right, that would help us a lot.

(Bristow et al., 2007, p. 55)

Participants identified a need for more money for staffing, particularly clerical and business staff who could take some of the load from them. The cohort also nominated negative staff issues, parental issues and bureaucracy as connected strongly with lack of job satisfaction (these are discussed in forthcoming chapters).

A similar study undertaken in 2003 in Victoria, Australia (Saulwick Muller Social Research, 2004), showed long hours of work taken up by increased demands for paperwork and report writing, a perceived conflict between the managerial and educational role with inadequate clerical and student welfare support. These studies, and others like them (e.g. Starr, 2001), show that while hours of headteacher work may have increased, or even increased and declined slightly, it is as much *what* headteachers do that is at issue as the actual time spent on work. Indeed, the continuity of evidence about headteachers' concerns about the encroachment of administrative and managerial tasks at the expense of the educational, and the time that this takes, suggests that Southworth's hope – that this was a transition stage where there were understandable concerns about changes in the job – may in fact be wishful thinking.

What we see is that the necessary everyday work of encounters documented by Wolcott has had added to it, over time, a pantechnicon of paperwork.

How do we understand why changed work matters?

It is important to understand why working long hours has become much more of a problem when it wasn't so much of an issue in the 1970s, when hours were nearly as long. The work has changed – but so what?

There are various ways of understanding why heads complain about changes in their work. These also help to explain the satisfaction paradox. When surveyed, headteachers invariably report high levels of job satisfaction (Bristow *et al.*, 2007; Chaplain, 2001; Mercer, 1997; National Secondary Principals' Associations, 2007; Saulwick Muller Social Research, 2004). Expressions of commitment to headship often occur in the very same studies as discontent with long hours and dissatisfaction with many aspects of the work. This apparent contradiction is not as silly as it might first appear.

One explanation is that heads are perfectionists and their own worst enemies (National Secondary Principals' Associations, 2007), but there are other ways to approach this conundrum.

Heads love the job, hate the work

Some research (e.g. Gini, 2001) points to the different meanings attached to the term job and work. Job is taken to mean an occupation, a profession, a calling. In the case of headteachers this means what might be called their mission, moral purpose or commitment to making a difference in the lives of young people. On the other hand, work is understood as encompassing the expectations of the job, the roles that are required and the everyday tasks that are involved. Dissatisfaction arises when there is a significant disconnection or conflict between the job and the work.

If headship is not merely a job, but is also 'the articulation and implementation of ... personal beliefs' (Southworth, 1995, p. 125), then it is understandable that heads will be concerned about hours of work spent on something that they do not value (see Box 4.4, Keith's story). It is possible that when asked about satisfaction heads will report on the job, but when asked about work, they respond to that as a different question.

Balancing the good, the bad and the ugly

Pounder and Merrill (2001) argue that people evaluate headship through three domains: (1) subjective (the desire to influence students and schools); (2) objective (remuneration, working conditions, time demands); and (3) critical contact (professional networking). They argue that one domain does not cancel the other out. Prospective and serving heads evaluate the headship through each domain to determine which dominates. If adverse conditions in the objective domain appear to delimit what might be achieved in the subjective domain, then they will be dissuaded from application, or dissatisfied if they are in the position (see Box 4.4). It could thus well be the case that questions about job satisfaction direct attention to the subjective features of the work, while those about work focus attention on the objective.

Box 4.4 Keith's story[2]

[W]e couldn't get a handle on the school's finances and we had this debt hanging over our heads and the department was only prepared to lend us $80,000 and what we had to do was to really go out there and get into the-commercial world. I wasn't prepared for that, I'm not a business person, and we had to run commercial activities and we had to run commercial programmes. So we got money ... money for work for the dole schemes and because we were a registered training organization, we could offer programs at night-time and over the holidays for adults. The department kind of frowned on this activity but we just went ahead and did it and we took a large amount of money for managing projects, and so on, and this is one of the ways we started to rebuild the finances of the school. And the other way was that we did a lot of reconnaissance with schools that had gone into the pilot devolution project and we decided, after a lot of haggling, that we would go in, and the one-off incentive to go in was very, very useful to us in clearing up some of our financial problems.

And it was, I've got to say, something that I felt very uncomfortable about. It was a part of the role, that particular role that I wasn't prepared for and I was, I guess, astute enough to realize that the finances of the school didn't look right to me. We went through, the school had gone through, before my time and since my time, they're up to their 6th bursar in four and a half years, each of them have been saying, 'It's just too hard, you know, I don't get this, it's too hard and I'm going.' And we had some really good ones too, which frightened me a great deal. And then there was some paring back because we found we could only run programmes by hiring hourly paid instructors and we didn't have things like employment contracts and so I learnt very rapidly about those sorts of things. I found it very difficult to get the global budget unit in the department to pay much attention to help us with our accounts. They did eventually. We did discover how much money we didn't have and we did get our chartered accounts in order. That was a major relief, I must say, at that particular time.

But all of the time my focus wanted to be around the curriculum and educational aspects of the job and I was just totally diverted and I started to lose direction. Now I know this is just one school and I'm not sure how generalizable this is or how small components of this might turn up in other schools but if you take that finance component of the job, which was enough to keep you awake all night long and busy all day long, and then you add the other compounding issues (falling enrolment, aggressive competitor neighbouring school) and the need to press the flesh and be seen to be supporting and to be in classrooms and be in the yard and to be working with kids all day long and then to be pushing the paper after hours, it made for really intolerable days and, you know, weekends that were just spent recovering and then doing more work. When it got to the stage of actually going back into the school on a Sunday, even though I lived so far away, it was easier sometimes to go in than drag it all home and spending an awful length of time there each Sunday, you began to think you were actually living there and that then begins to have a kick-back in terms of your equilibrium, in terms of the way you tend to interact with people, become short-tempered … it certainly has an effect on marriage, there's no doubt about that, and has an effect on your own health. It certainly did for me.

So that's when I stopped and went on leave. It took me from the beginning of July to the middle of September, last year, to realize that I really didn't want to go back and do it any more. And I'm sure it wasn't just the ambience of Umbria at the time – that helps – but I'd discovered that I could structure my time differently, that I had control over that, that my health had improved, that I wasn't drinking as much and that was an issue, getting by each day with that bottle of red wine was important, and I'm not a great drinker, but it became important for me. And that I was able to read, and read for pleasure and I was able to enjoy art again and music and a whole lot of things and so I just made a decision that I wasn't going to go back.

And I didn't. So I extended my leave a little while and had a little talk to the district superintendent when I came back and he said, 'I understand.' Now I'm not sure *what* he understood but he understood that I wasn't going back anyhow.

(Keith, Australian secondary headteacher, retired).

From 1998 to 2004, Boris-Schacter and Langer (2006) asked over 200 principals from all regions of the United States why headship was unattractive and why heads were leaving their positions. They divided the answers into three polarities:

1 Instruction versus management.
2 Work versus personal lives.
3 Society/community expectations versus individual priorities and values.

Boris-Schacter and Langer argue that there must be a balance in each of the three areas. Failure to achieve balance in *each* of the three dissuades potential applicants and also produces dissatisfaction and stress among serving principals. This was clearly not Keith's experience (Box 4.4).

What I want or what they want

Leanne Perry, an Australian headteacher, researched her own workload (Perry, 2006). She wanted to see how much time she spent on 'performance goals' (those directed towards predetermined outcomes through the use and validation of existing capability) as opposed to 'learning goals' (those focused on learning, growth and extending capability). She reasoned that performance goals, determined by extrinsic requirements and needs, would be less meaningful to her, negatively affect her own sense of well-being and efficacy as well as potentially adversely influence the achievement of her own and organizational goals. Perry kept a record of all of the activities that she undertook in one week (see Box 4.5).

Perry found that performance goals dominated all categories of her work from management to pastoral domains. Her week was prescribed by the demonstration of externally determined outcomes, rather than being directed towards strategies for learning and improvement. She argues that her data show that her commitment to develop a learning organization was 'under

> **Box 4.5 Headteacher self-study**
>
> The work of the case study principal during the project week was dominated by activities involving human resources and pastoral and community building. The human resources activities during this week included the summative performance review of a person in a promotion position. This involved a panel interview process which included a panel briefing, a lengthy interview with the person being reviewed, a post-interview panel meeting, report writing, and a subsequent individual feedback meeting with the person being reviewed. A number of interviews for appointments to short-term acting promotion positions were also held during this week. In addition, a number of appointments for the principal held during this week with members of the Senior Executive and Middle Management related to human resource issues such as anticipated staffing changes, performance concerns and processional development planning. In the category of pastoral and community, a large proportion of the time was spent on informal interactions with members of the community – attendance at sporting carnivals, playground interactions, parent social evenings, tuckshop visits and the like. A funeral for a very long-serving recently retired member of staff was held during this week. Time spent attending the funeral and in conversation with both current and past members of the community as part of the grieving process were significant elements of this pastoral category.
>
> (Perry, 2006, Project, p. 17)

pressure from an externally driven regulatory regime' (ibid., p. 23). She suggests that this pressure militated against her taking the kinds of risks that are necessary for learning, in favour of managing possible risks of failure and harm. This kind of disjunction produces internal conflict between satisfaction derived from intrinsic learning goals and the achievement of performance goals.

Keeping out of harm's way

The development of the 'risk society' has produced organizational and individual practices in which the minimization of harm and the rational management of a world under control dominate everyday life in schools and professional modes of knowing and being (McWilliam and Singh, 2004). Headteachers are no exception to this and they have no choice but to address systemic risks – they must avoid bringing public disapproval to both the school and the government. Heads are directed to avoid:

1 the risks of failing to improve;
2 the risks of failing to show that funds have been spent wisely, to show that they operate safely, efficiently and effectively.

Headteacher dissatisfaction might well arise from the overemphasis on the negative rather than the positive logic of risk. Questions about job satisfaction focus responses on the creative elements of the work, while questions about the work reveal headteachers' frustration with its negative risk avoidance.

'It ain't me babe'

In collaborative research into the declining supply of school principals in Australia, Blackmore, Sachs and I conducted interviews with system leaders, principals, principals' professional organizations and union officials (Blackmore *et al.*, 2005). A set of key phrases emerged in our data: these were testament to the idea that many believed that the work – and identity – of the principal were increasingly unattractive to some teachers. State system officials told us that teachers were not applying for principal positions because they could no longer 'see themselves' in the job. Union officers suggested that deteriorating industrial relations meant that many teachers felt that if they applied for principal's positions, they would have 'joined the others', 'left teachers behind' and 'become someone they don't want to be'. Some of our respondents suggested that teachers did not want 'to be the kind of person' who spent large amounts of time dealing with complaints and litigious parents, paperwork and meetings. These statements are indicative of the interconnection between work and identity and its role in decision-making.

Wenger (1998) offers one way of understanding this connection. He proposes that organizations such as school systems and schools are sites in which there are 'communities of practice'. He suggests that belonging to particular communities and actively engaging in their joint enterprises is the process through which community members come to have ownership of particular ways of being and doing things. There is, of course, a historical dimension to communities of practice. If the identity formed in one community of practice becomes enmeshed in new forms of practice grafted onto the older ones, then there is potential for conflict between the required selves. This, we reasoned, was what we were being told by our interviewees was the case. The prime identity of heads was that of teacher, whereas more recent performative management requirements produced them as managers with little direct pedagogical engagement with students, and with less and less time for educational work and thinking. Questions about job satisfaction were answered by the primary teacherly identity, which also commented on the hours and nature of work expected of the newer managerial self.

The consequences of over, under, upside-down work

Any one of the five reasons outlined above is sufficient to show that overwork and the changed nature of work produce deeply experienced tensions and contradictions. While these cause dissatisfaction for many, the burden of living with them everyday may be sufficiently grave to cause some heads to leave. They may also act as a disincentive to application for those who can see heads at work.

There are serious consequences of overwork (see Box 4.6). In 2003, the suicide of a primary headteacher, Jeff Barger, featured in the Australian newspaper, *The Age*.[3] The article detailed the overwhelming workload which kept Barger away from family and friends and then highlighted the plight of those who suffered depression as a result of working too hard and too long without respite. Subsequent print media articles linked the lack of applications for school principal positions to the Barger suicide, tangible evidence it was claimed, of the increasingly difficult, onerous and tricky business of school leadership (see Box 4.6).

These suicides are the tip of the proverbial iceberg. One recent Australian study (National Secondary Principals' Associations, 2007) reported that a majority of heads felt guilty about the work they had failed to complete, were concerned about the effects on their families, and became increasingly disenchanted the longer they were in the job (Mercer, 1997, also found a connection with time in post). A third of survey respondents reported that they had a diagnosed medical condition, nearly half of this was cardio-vascular problems: about a fifth reported psychological and another fifth gastro-intestinal problems. Nearly half also reported that they slept badly. These kinds of illnesses are highly likely to be occupationally linked and stress-related. Less dramatic but also alarming is a 2007 survey (Angle *et al.*, 2007) which showed that only 7 per cent of secondary heads in England felt able to pursue any interests outside of work.

Box 4.6 Dying for and in the job

The demands and pressures on principals is (*sic*) increasing all the time, Ratledge said. 'I saw a poll recently that ranks principals as having the highest suicide rate, second to police officers,' he said. 'You're being pulled at from all directions.'
(*The Daily Times*, 24 August 2002, www.thedailytimes.com/sited/story/html/ 102959; accessed 28 September 2002)

An elementary school principal who spent almost half of his life as an educator in Prince William County was found dead in a park Monday ... Prince William officers said they were investigating his death as a suicide ... School officials said yesterday that Drummond usually arrived at school at 6 am to get his administrative work done so he could spend the rest of his time with students.
(*Washington Post*, 7 November 2007 www.washington post.com/wp-dyn/ content/article/2007/11/06/AR200711060285.html; accessed 3 December 2007)

I return to the question of stress in the last two chapters of the book. For now it is sufficient to note that overwork can have serious personal consequences. And, it is important to ask, as prospective heads may well do – why do something that makes you ill?

There is *abundant* evidence that most headteachers not only work long hours, but that what they do during that time has changed over time. These changes are a source of tension and concern for many in the position and they appear to be a significant deterrent for potential applicants. Those who are in post may well feel themselves engaged in activities which risk their health and well-being, while some of those who look at the job as a possible career move assess this as a risk too far.

In the next chapter I look at some aspects of headteachers' work which make great demands on them. These are not necessarily causes of overwork or stress, but, just like the matter of time on task, the risks attached to them may well be connected with the supply problem in important ways.

Chapter 5

Head land

The problem of the time-consuming and predictable

Zoe Heller's (2003) novel and subsequent film, *Notes on a Scandal*, turns on an illegal relationship between a teacher and a student and a destructive relationship between the teacher and one of her colleagues. The upshot is that the 'naughty' teacher is prosecuted and her colleague 'persuaded' to retire. While fictional, this event has parallels in real schools. It is what I call a predictable issue. However, unlike Heller, I want to focus sympathetically on the head who must deal with this and other predictable issues.

Most schools have the same number of people in them as small villages. It is hardly surprising that crises and difficulties arise simply from having so many together in one place over an extended period of time. People inevitably get sick, have accidents, squabble, are nasty to each other, do not follow rules, and some do very bad things. Headteachers are quite rightly expected, and they expect, to deal with such things. However, this has become harder of late.

Headteachers with devolved responsibilities can generally rely on local authorities/school districts for advice, but they must take full responsibility for what happens on their sites. The general public now assumes that it is right and proper for them to know what goes on at all times in all places to all people, and that it is acceptable to take legal action if there appears to be a dereliction of public duty. Heads have thus found that what goes on in their schools is increasingly subject to public judgement, media attention and litigious claims.

These kinds of everyday management issues feature heavily in head-teachers' professional association newsletters and training sessions, but they are not often discussed in the latest leadership literatures, perhaps because they were the stuff of yesterday's management training. They do, however, often form part of 'problem-based' training programmes (e.g. Hallinger and Bridges, 2007) and they are inevitably raised by aspiring and new heads when they get the opportunity to determine what they want to discuss. It is important to note at the start of this chapter that predictable issues are not discussed nearly often enough in relation to questions of the desirability or otherwise of the job (Boris-Schacter and Langer, 2006, are an exception).

While no-one experiences all of the possible issues associated with everyday headship, many heads experience quite a few. This chapter describes some of the most common, and addresses not only the effects that they have in schools but also their impact on headteachers themselves.

Groundhog Day: predictable issues

In this chapter, I focus on only three predictable issues that are basic to the operation of schools, those to do with: (1) staff; (2) plant and buildings; and (3) dealing with a troubled and troubling minority of families. Together, these can consume vast amounts of time and energy.

Staffing matters

An NCSL study of headteachers' work (Bristow *et al.*, 2007) claimed that 39 per cent of headteachers' time was taken up with staffing matters, building, budgets and the like. Of these, heads reported that by far the most time-consuming and difficult was giving negative feedback to staff.

It is often the range and nature of issues with staff that surprise people new to senior management the most, and this surprise marks the gulf between the deputy position and the head. Much of what happens during the most difficult staffing transactions is confidential, so it is hardly surprising that many deputies are shocked when they find out the extent and nature of staffing predicaments.

Routine staffing matters that require the heads' time include the following:

- *Getting the right staff.* All heads know that getting the right staff for the school is vital. Without a critical mass of well-trained, interested and hard-working teachers, nothing good happens. Some schools more than others have difficulty attracting staff. Where this is the case heads often find themselves in the situation of having to: (1) decide whether appointing the one applicant is better than having no teacher at all; (2) depend on a number of overseas teachers who can and will only stay a relatively short period of time; (3) appoint a good 'cover teacher' to the post, thus creating a knock-on problem in cover; and/or (4) decide how much time and effort to put into advertising the post versus galvanizing the teacher 'grapevine'.
- *Supporting all staff to teach well.* Some heads must face a situation where they have a full complement of staff, but not all are ready/prepared/able to move forward in the way that is required. Dealing with this kind of situation can be very difficult (see Box 5.1) as heads must make wise decisions about who will respond to new leadership opportunities, who needs a little pressure, who needs encouragement to move on, and

Box 5.1 Getting the right staff with the right stuff

{W}e have had a lot of turnover – but very healthy turnover because what it's done is to galvanize the people who are there and we've been able to recruit some really high quality people but we've also been very clear for the people who weren't on board. And that has made life much more pleasant for everybody else because we've got rid of the BMWs – bloody-minded whiners – those who are constantly moaning about some gripe or other. And the really incompetent people as well. I'm very fortunate in that I've never had to take anybody to 'capability', because the people who knew that they couldn't hack the expectations have actually got on their bikes and gone. And that has been very good for the other staff to see.

But there are a couple of staff this year that I have real concerns about and I'm thinking, what do we do? They're negative; they are potentially quite disruptive and influential and kind of like the hard core. So what do we do? And one guy in particular wants to get a climbing wall built and stuff like that and I've given him a post and he's got responsibility for it and now he wants to take on extra stuff. So he's totally changed in the last few months from the person he was last year so when you see that happen and you see people's way of working change and their practice develop, it does give you a sense of achievement and that you are actually really going forward.

(New secondary head, UK)

who must be monitored and may end up in some kind of competency proceedings.

• *Being supportive and also compliant with set procedures.* Headteachers expect to spend time working with staff on developing the craft of teaching, but this now often means using particular kinds of observation and supervision routines demanded by audit requirements. Mike Kent, headteacher of Comber Grove Primary in Camberwell, writing in the *Times Educational Supplement* (21 September 2007, p. 33) takes issue with paper-driven systems of performance management. He was recommended by OfSTED to conduct formal assessments of staff without which he could not demonstrate he had a system for monitoring teaching and learning:

> So for half a term I did just that. I became an inspector rather than a resource, and I learned nothing about my teachers and classrooms that I didn't know already. Then I went back to doing what I knew worked best.

Kent asserts that the problem with performance management is that it is a system which lacks trust in teachers. A breakout box in the column says, 'What I refuse to do is sit in the corner of a classroom ticking boxes on the teacher's performance.' Most heads, however, do what is required and do not exercise this kind of resistance.

Headteachers *do* now spend more time than ever before on routine observation. They also, as Box 5.1 suggests, spend time recruiting and moving on teachers who don't meet the school's aspirations and needs. This is totally predictable work – as predictable is the likelihood that at some point in their careers the vast majority of heads will need to take action on the competence of a member of staff.

Dealing with 'incompetence'

There are considerable pressures on heads to be seen to be doing something about 'poor teaching'. Heads, teachers and parents in England were recently greeted by headlines asserting that there were up to 17,000 'incompetent teachers' in the system. The head of the Specialist Schools and Academies Trust, Sir Cyril Taylor was working from estimates of the numbers of teachers who were not reported as 'good' by OfSTED, that is they were 'poor' teachers who failed to produce under observation the required four-part lesson with explicit targets. This estimate was then taken up by the head of the General Teaching Council, the body responsible for maintaining teaching standards in England who said:

> It is not unreasonable to assume that in a workforce of half a million there is a proportion that is probably around 17,000 that are in practice sub-standard … It's probably not the incompetent teachers who are the problem. It's teachers who are struggling with their classrooms day in, day out – part of that is behaviour management in increasingly difficult classrooms.
>
> (*Guardian*, 4 February 2008)[1]

Research on teacher incompetence suggests that the number of teachers who are incompetent is actually very small (Bridges, 1986, 1992). The English General Teaching Council has in its seven-year history only barred eight teachers from working in schools although it suggests that schools and local authorities are failing to report other cases. Of the 27 disciplinary cases it heard in the first three months of 2008,[2] nine were criminal offences, and only two arose from poor teaching practices – inadequate record keeping and marking of students' assessments. The majority of offences were associated with teaching rather than arising directly from it – misuse of ICT facilities, inappropriate relations with students, misuse of funds. And Googling 'teacher sacked' produces a number of examples of teacher misdemeanour, only a minority of which are related to actual classroom teaching. Nevertheless, the general public, (mis)informed by media, must surely assume that schools are full of disastrous teachers. It is hardly surprising that participatory educational blogs contain numerous suggestions about teacher incompetence and sacking.

Heads generally do not have to deal with sacking offences. Nor do they most often see incompetence in classroom teaching, but rather teaching which could and should be better, just as the head of the GTC suggested.

Dealing with teaching which could be better often requires ongoing and formal intervention which is emotionally draining and time-consuming for all concerned. Sometimes this extends to formal procedures which require the development of a written plan with stated objectives for improvement (see Box 5.2). While these kinds of processes can make a difference, sometimes they do not. Teachers hover in a kind of limbo, not incompetent, but seemingly unable to do what is required to do better. At such a point, heads question their own competence, and under new forms of school inspection and self-evaluation, it may also be queried by others (see Chapter 7).

A small Australian practitioner study (Elsworth, 2007) of headteachers' experiences of 'improvement' procedures claims that: heads were 'deeply driven to conduct teacher underperformance management procedures as a result of their own professional values and ethics and not because of systemic expectations' (ibid., p. 3); the procedures required 'significant extra allocations of finance, time and human support from school budgets ... normally allocated to previously planned teaching/learning school priorities' (ibid., p. 4); and heads showed

Box 5.2 The required procedures for teacher improvement

With the full support of the central office and school board, we developed a plan and began a three-month period of intensive supervision, during which time two special education supervisors and I would provide assistance and resources. The plan included frequent conferences in which we would provide Ms Jackson with feedback and suggestions for implementing effective teaching practices ... but although she expressed a strong desire to improve, her desire did not translate into improved performance. About once a week I went to her classroom to observe, hoping to see some kind of improved teaching skills, only to be disappointed. Watching her failure was agonizing to me. Time and again, I would return to my office, close the door, and fight back tears of frustration ... she failed to return to the classroom for the last six weeks of the school year and for the first semester of the following year. Claiming that she was ill and on medication for depression she requested one and half years of sick leave, which was denied.

(Experienced primary head, USA, quoted in Blacklock, 2002)

moral responsibility to their school communities; determination to protect students and teachers from psychological and emotional traumas; tenacity to achieve quality learning outcomes for students; and self-respect from their own sense of purpose and role … all at significant cost to their own psychological, emotional, physical and professional well-being.

Elsworth argues that heads experience 'paradoxical roles of being a supporter/ mentor for teachers responsible for developing a professional, co-operative, accountable workforce while also expected to identify and manage under- performing teachers according to systemic accountability expectations and legislation requirements' (ibid., p. 1). She reports that heads in her study experienced a set of stress-related illnesses arising from extended involvement in these kinds of procedures.

It is my experience that teachers carefully observe whether their heads humanely and quickly influence the teaching quality of those peers who they know to be struggling. This certainly influences their view of the position.

Dealing with staffing crises

Most heads are likely to encounter at least one critical staffing incident in their career. In her book, *Teachers Behaving Badly* (2005), Kate Myers addresses such incidents in detail. She names misconduct or incompetence, personal and/or professional life as being the cause of crises, and possible actions as either advice and counselling, or suspension and formal investigation.

Personal issues are often the hardest to deal with – the mental illness of a teacher, alcoholism, a devastating family crisis which affects performance. When these affect students, there is evidence to be acted on (see Box 5.3). In many instances, heads have suspicions about personal problems, and must then go about a long and complex process of investigation. Acting prematurely, even to offer advice, runs the risk of accusations of unfairness, bullying, pro- ducing stress. Due process *is* what is required and heads are committed to it. But there are very few situations worse for heads, particularly when there are students at stake, than being sure something potentially damaging to pro- fessional duties is going on, and not having enough evidence to act.[3]

Both giving advice and initiating and implementing formal processes can be very difficult and require a great deal of skill, judgment and patience. They can also be incredibly long term (see Box 5.4).

Such issues can create divisions in the staff. Colleagues often have limited information, personal loyalties and strongly held views. When a critical inci- dent occurs, heads are generally unable to do more than send out a carefully worded statement about events and proceedings. They are *always* unable to share their personal feelings of fear, inadequacy, stress and/or anger. They must simply work with the disquiet in their school community and do their best to reassure everyone that due process is occurring.

Box 5.3 Dealing with a critical staffing incident

I had a member of staff have a breakdown, a proper, full-blown one. I mean, you went to her house and the furniture was in the garden and all the course work. Well, we picked up all the paper we could find and brought it back but that was all the class's coursework gone and the teacher was too ill to help sort it out ... it was all plastered on the front page of the local paper ... I was being approached by people in the street when I was out at the weekend with my family ... we'd worked with the exam board so it wouldn't have impacted on students ... but that wasn't the point for them and all of this investigation is still working through ... Theoretically, I might have to go to court to talk about that ... that rumbled on for a bit and the leader of the council and politicians were giving me grief ... my MP is not short of a word when he needs it – so there was quite a lot of pressure there. Physically, I've been fine but mentally I've been stressed. I find, as a head, I couldn't share those stresses with the staff. So you have to carry it on your own in school and carry on with your job but it's hard to get through that.

(Secondary head, UK)

Box 5.4 Time taken for disciplinary issues

There was a difficult disciplinary where we moved to dismissal because there was a teacher who had an inappropriate relationship with a student so we went for dismissal ... I was very reliant on HR advice about that ... and we made a mistake. So the teacher went for appeal and HR were also advising the governors and they said that they needed to overturn the dismissal otherwise this could end up as a tribunal – it was on a technicality. So it got overturned and then it took two years to resolve. The member of staff is not here now but I was subject to a grievance around several claims of harassment ... and that was a huge chunk of my time.

One of the hearings went on for six hours. The investigation involved interviewing twelve children and their families which were all transcribed so it was a huge amount of work. And then the case notes were about fifty pages and there have been a couple of times since where I've actually taken the easy option on a disciplinary – but of course not where it's a child protection thing. But the amount of time it takes is quite hard.

And then the member of staff was going to come back to school and then a child on the corridor told me that the member of staff was coming back to school before we'd had a meeting so, clearly, this member of staff was still in an inappropriate relationship so, eventually, we came to a mutual termination but it took the best part of two years. And also they were on full pay for the whole time. So it was incredibly draining ... and also the union rep was like a rottweiler and it was quite personal and I was unprepared for that.

I'd not done anything like that before because usually disciplinaries don't get to that stage, because people tend to come to an agreement earlier on so I'd never actually gone through that before, and I was quite surprised because I thought that, yes, you had to ensure that the teacher had protection – but it was a child protection issue and it seemed to me that we should be behaving in the way that protected the child and the school but it didn't feel like that. It felt like a court-room drama ... one that went on for two years.

(Secondary head, UK)

There simply is no option for heads but to spend time on staffing matters, be they disciplinary or recruitment, or simply a question of improvement. Heads simultaneously rate this as one of the most important tasks they do, but also the most trying and difficult area. It is also an area which prospective heads may well wish to avoid.

Bog standard issues with buildings

Headteachers worry about buildings. They know that the kind of environment in which teachers work and students learn makes a real difference. New heads routinely make changes to the physical environment when they first take up post, and heads appointed to 'failing' schools generally see such changes as key to changing expectations and patterns of behaviour (see Box 5.5).

Together with less than tasty and affordable food and buses that run late, almost nothing is guaranteed to create daily disquiet more than problems with the plumbing. Ian Kaplan (2008) reports on a 'student voice' project in which special education students took photographs of toilets in their school. They interpreted poor toilet facilities as a sign that the school did not care about them and their welfare. The deputy head refused to allow the students to present the photographs to the whole staff since they showed the school in a bad light, but did allow a modified version, after which there was a school-wide review of toilet provision. The project was thus partially successful but it revealed some of the sensitivities that the school administration felt over its capacity to manage its plant in the interests of its students. It was clearly an area of some perceived vulnerability. This is not uncommon. Most heads experience a set of mundane concerns about plant, and inevitably these are to do with the wiring, heating, cooling and plumbing. None of these constitute a significant crisis in themselves but they do add to duties that can overtake educational issues.

> **Box 5.5 Paying attention to the building**
>
> We've made quite a lot of changes in terms of improving the building and improving the quality of the learning environment and the quality of the resources available to students and staff. This is a school with a reasonably healthy budget as compared to some and yet there just didn't seem to have been any investment in the staff or in the people. If you don't invest, then how do you expect people to feel valued?
>
> (New secondary head)
>
> Franciso is entranced at the idea of brightening up the school. He brings in paint charts and he and I spend a happy lunch hour going over them together ... we decide to give the corridors priority, and choose a different colour for each floor – a sunshine yellow, a brilliant red, and a very bright blue. I call them 'McDonald's colours', the sort of colours I know young people like ... There are probably a dozen official channels to go through, and I should have spent hours debating with various agencies, but we're now so excited we want to start now, so I give Francisco the go-head to buy the paint. The Governors have been extremely helpful about releasing money from their funds, for which I'm grateful. But, 'Well, it's the children's money anyway,' I think.
>
> (Stubbs, 2003, p. 75)

Toilets are not generally discussed in literature about the work that heads do, yet they can take up enormous amounts of time and energy. Any serving headteacher knows that toilets are not a trivial matter. A minority of students often become enamoured of vandalizing toilets or of using them for smoking or plotting nefarious activities. Their peers, disgusted by the condition of the toilets, afraid of the occupants, or simply embarrassed to use them, justifiably have complaints, as do their parents. They call into question the school's discipline competence: if the school has good discipline how come the toilets keep getting vandalized? But common school responses – use of signed-out keys or the more modern CCTV – are also not acceptable to many students and their parents. The answer, of course, lies in a much more complex set of negotiations about collective responsibility and as such, it is hardly surprising that School Councils UK has toilets as one of their campaigning issues, since toilets are not only a basic health and hygiene issue but a flash point around which the ways in which the school-as-village lives and works together. Dealing with the fall-out that surrounds decisions about toilets can be wearying and challenging.

Blocked plumbing is a different kind of problem for heads, and one which can have serious consequences if not attended to quickly. If one block of toilets is out of action, then students can usually be accommodated. If all of them are dysfunctional, then there is little option but for someone (in big schools not generally the head) to engage in a frantic ring-around to plumbers. If one is not rapidly available, permission to close the school must be obtained. But parents have to be notified in such cases, and many students who cannot go home have to be supervised and ferried to nearby public or other schools' toilets when they need them. The next day will almost inevitably bring post-closure complaints. Aging school buildings often have chronic problems with plumbing and such incidents can come relatively frequently. This may reach crisis level with parents and governors quite reasonably concerned about health and safety. However, as Box 5.6 suggests, plumbing problems also come with new buildings.

Technically, in most public education systems, the local authority/school district is the purchaser of buildings, not schools. Yet, as in Box 5.6, the authorities are sometimes reluctant to shoulder this responsibility. This is often because of new funding arrangements.

Box 5.6 Plumbing problems

On our first day in the school there is some problem in one of the toilet blocks (there are four in the school) and because of drainage issues in the hall where dinners are eaten, the children ate dinners outside amid the rain showers. By the second day the problem has spread: the two toilets closest to the office are closed down. In morning assembly the head tells the children about the problem and reminds the boys, who no longer have access to urinals, to wee down the toilet and not on the floor – 'or it will be dreadful' she says, wrinkling her nose.

The head spends much of her time on the first day and the beginning of the second trying to get someone to attend to the problem. The building contractor won't take responsibility, refuses to come out and refers it back to her. The LA keep referring her to the contractor and reminding her that the building has been handed over and that she is responsible for maintenance. She finally manages to get an obliging young plumber to come out. 'Tell me I can close the school,' she says to him in the staff room in everyone's hearing. He diagnoses the problem as being building waste blocking pipes.

During explorations of the school sewerage system, he locates the remains of an old Victorian toilet which we are invited to see – we don't go. It seems the new build has used some of the plumbing from the previous one rather than re-sewer the site. In order to fix the problem, the plumber has to lift the carpet in the new staff room and dig up a piece of concrete. Not only has the carpet contractor glued down where he shouldn't but also the person who laid the floor secured the trap to the sewer rather too securely. The plumber tells the head he is not a builder or carpet layer and she gives permission for him to do the whole job, mindful that if anything isn't up to scratch, there will be no come-back. The staff room is closed between recess and lunch, a rather dreadful smell flushed out of the room, and it and the toilets are reopened at lunch-time.

The head tells us that this is not the first such incident since the school took control of the new building in September last year. It is actually the eighth plumbing problem in seven months. The head says she has never worked for such a bad local authority – they have been remarkably silent about the plumbing and other building issues. Only once has she been rung – and then by the 'well-being officer' to see how she was coping ... she was insulted by this, she reports. She needed plumbers, not sympathy.

(UK field notes, 2007: primary head now resigned)

In England, as in Canada, PFI (Private Finance Initiatives) have created new requirements for school plant – their use, maintenance, improvement and cleaning (see Ball, 2007, for details of the extent of PFIs in the UK). It is becoming apparent that there are some relatively predictable consequences arising from some of these arrangements for schools and their heads. Not only can it be difficult to get anyone to take responsibility for problems, but also with PFI buildings, the head may be stuck with inflexible *per capita* costings and chains of agencies responsible for various aspects of plant use. School budgets for maintenance, small additional improvements and cleaning are no longer simply the heads' decision, but are subject to contractual agreements. Heads in such situations do not have the autonomy to make a decision to allow a plumber to do a job as did the head in Box 5.6. Rather, they must use specified contractors with specifically demarcated jobs. Heads in PFI buildings may find themselves paying a *per capita* cleaning cost which is higher than their falling enrolments, but which is fixed in a contract. They may find themselves having to go through a range of agencies to build a pergola rather than hiring one of the students' fathers who has a pergola building business, and paying much more as a result. They may find themselves unable to use the school for community events, since a contract stipulates that it can be let out to commercial users out of school hours.[4] This puts them administratively back prior to school devolution, to a time when plant and buildings were beyond their control.

But even apparently unproblematic new builds where local authorities act responsibly, and where contractors are helpful, can have significant consequences as Box 5.7 demonstrates.

This experience is not atypical and care for students ought to be, as the head in Box 5.7 suggests, built into the planning of renovation programmes. After all, many of us know how disruptive it is to live in a house undergoing

Box 5.7 The effects of new buildings

We went for a build which cost eleven-and-a-half million and the government gave us eight-and-a-half. So you're left with a really tight programme and there is no money in there to really compensate the school for the disruption ... we involved students fantastically well in the design and there have been some fantastic bits that the students have created.

Once we started, the big constraint was the programme: every week on site cost fifteen thousand pounds. The constructors were saying: 'Oh can't do that, mate.' So you've got to make a decision about the twenty-five years that this school building is designed for versus the needs of the children in that year. And it's a rock and a hard place. Every little decision that you make has an impact and you don't know till afterwards, sometimes, quite what the impact is.

If Tesco were to rebuild, their first priority is not to impact on customers. So one of our key things was that our attendance dropped by over 2 per cent in the year of build because we had to take out the student entrance. The alternative would have been to put a solid roof on it so they could come in safely but that would have cost a lot of money and it wasn't in the programme. But Tesco wouldn't have baulked at that. So we had to send the students down the road, up the back and round the field and it was awful. And I stood at the gate and I watched them go to the end and to the roundabout and go right – the opposite way from school!

What happened a year ago was that the kids were just fed up. I mean, talk about student voice: we were talking to them and doing things with them but, somehow, we didn't hear or perhaps they didn't express it properly or perhaps they didn't know. When we did an exit survey with the Year 11, the disenchantment they expressed about the constant upheaval that the building works caused was intense. And our results dropped last year to 20 per cent.

It is my third direct experience of a building programme and I'm probably more experienced than most but ... our results plummeted so I got it wrong ... by definition. And yet I know that we could have protected the kids and done more for them and I would have lost a big chunk of the new build and where would we be now?

At the time it's not clear ... the other thing with building programmes is that they come in and it all has to be done now. I mean, I built in that they had to give me a day's grace but you are still under a lot of pressure. You often have twenty-four hours to make a decision ... more or less. And I'm not a builder. I mean, I seconded somebody to do all the day-to-day stuff but the big decisions had to be made by me. And when it finished, we were late in opening and in having the full hand-over and then OfSTED arrived three weeks afterwards.

> And while they were sympathetic, the school was in a worse place than it had been and we were working hard to bring students back into place and behaviour was not as good at it had been. And from what OfSTED saw and according to their criteria, they could not have done anything else.
> But the building *is* fantastic and our results are now going back up.
> (Specialist college headteacher, UK)

renovations, and it doesn't take much imagination to realize that the same thing will happen in schools, only writ on a much larger scale. This is a good example of a predictable risk which seems to have evaded those responsible for funding and contractual management.

Many heads of course just *dream* of such problems. Living with staffrooms that are too small for the current staff complement, temporary classrooms that have been *in situ* for decades, inadequate storage, no meeting rooms, aging wiring, leaking roofs, heating that doesn't work, lack of cooling, lack of space for teachers to prepare, no sick rooms, grounds that are too small – these are things that cause ongoing discomfort and low-key grumpiness. Despite the best will of education systems – and in England, for example, there is a very serious commitment to replacing such buildings – it is heads who must cope with waiting in line.

These examples about toilets and buildings are only illustrative. Building problems range from the predictable issues of routine maintenance, to equally predictable but less frequent occurrences concerning serious maintenance and renovation. What might not be anticipated is a combination of shoddy work and a failure of the appropriate body to take responsibility. All three take their toll on headteachers, but only the unanticipated ought not to figure in job and role descriptions. Plant issues ought not to be dismissed and disconnected from the school's educational mission or the head's everyday work.

Troubled and troubling families

Unlike most villages, schools *expect* to be heavily engaged in the processes of keeping order, because part of their job is to educate children and young people to learn to be citizens of their own school-village, and the wider world beyond the school gates.

Handling dis-order is part of everyday life in schools and is usually called 'discipline' or 'behaviour management'. Most schools do have well-developed systems for teaching and maintaining order, and for dealing with those children and young people who take a little longer than others to learn how to conform. Testing out the consequences, and pushing for independence are part and parcel of growing up, and good, inclusive schools know how to accommodate and nurture free spirits. But even in the most well-ordered village there are some who, for various combinations of individual and social-economic reasons, fail to stick to the rules (see Box 5.8).

It is not my intention to detail why such behaviours occur, or to suggest what can be done about them. Rather, it is to point to the kinds of demands it makes on heads. Their tasks in relation to ongoing disruption by children and young people, or their families, are: (1) to ensure that the disciplinary and welfare systems are well staffed, clear and effective; (2) to support staff through professional development; and (3) to ensure that the school uses appropriate supplementary services when needed. They also must take up those instances when only the head will do; (4) to be the end-point of disciplinary encounters; and (5) to take on the most difficult and/or urgent cases of ongoing trouble.

Those who are troubled and troubling are a tiny minority of the school community, but dealing with them can take hours and hours of time. In previous research (Thomson, 2002), I suggested that some schools ('disadvantaged', 'challenging', 'urban') had to deal with more of these kinds of families than others, because of the pressures caused by poverty. I showed that up to a third of available leadership and management time could regularly be swallowed up in working with very few children and families. While extended services can shoulder responsibility for ongoing support for

Box 5.8 A minority of parents

As is probably the case with most principals, I have had at least one student whose behaviour has been repeatedly disruptive, antisocial, and occasionally dangerous. Our discipline system involves parents as much as they are able and willing to cooperate, but one father had bucked me and the system constantly. One morning, in response to what had become a series of discipline notices, this father roared into our school parking lot via the exit, screeched to a halt in the bus loading zone, and stomped into my office demanding to see me. I gave him time to calm down by feigning a phone call but when I finally bade goodbye to the receiver and rose to greet him, he only become more angry. I tried to interject reason and diplomacy between his epithets and threats of everything from lawsuits to my pending need for plastic surgery. Frustrated by his failure to persuade me of the justice of his cause, the man swung a fist in my face. Before he left the building, I called the police to notify them I had been publicly threatened with personal and property injury ... The next time I saw the man, however, the first thing he did was apologise for his words and actions that day.

(Wilkens, 1995, p. 58)

some, handling the immediate issues which lead to such interventions, and managing the processes of accessing interagency provision, still mean work for heads and others in the senior management team.

This is personally as well as professionally demanding work for heads, just as it is for teachers, and each finds their own way of understanding and approaching it (see Box 5.9). There are often difficult ethical issues with pedagogical implications at stake (Evans, 1999): the head requires wisdom and good luck in equal measure in order to make a fair and just decision.

Box 5.9 Coming to terms with trouble

Even primary children can do outrageous things, from stealing to bullying – one boy severely beat up a girl after school and landed her in hospital. And general nastiness, implacable defiance and rudeness, and dangerous or crazy behaviour are not unknown. One girl set a boy's woolly on fire. Twenty girls formed a thieving consortium and robbed a local shop of much of its stock: they then traded the goods on a school blackmarket … It is all as much a test of the teacher as the child. There are many hazards, such as the real danger of over-reacting to what the child has done, and becoming over-emotional and over-punitive, and getting almost everything out of perspective. Teachers – indeed almost anybody – can fall victim, when angry enough, to a paranoia that splits the world into good and evil, black and white, mirroring, as it happens, the disturbed behaviour of children. A righteous anger can sometimes sweep down and block out all commonsense. Sometimes I could feel it inside myself.

(Winkley, 2002, pp. 110, 115)

No course in college or graduate school can adequately prepare you to deal with the human side of leadership. This is especially true in today's public schools, where, sad to say, hostile parents, clueless supervisors, and incompetent complainers are not uncommon. A school leader who is focused on her mission of helping kids is likely to find herself caught off guard by the assaults of these negative people. I'm not speaking here of well-intentioned people who happen to disagree with you, but of people who, for whatever reason are actively interested in impeding your work and who cannot be appealed to on any rational basis. It takes only a few such people to severely disrupt the life of a school. If the leader cannot outthink and, when necessary outcrazy those who try to attack her or her staff, the mission may be imperiled. If the leader backs down or crumbles before an assault, word will quickly spread throughout the school and community: 'You can get what you want if you threaten or act loud.' Once that perception takes hold, you're in trouble.

(Monroe, 1997, pp. 160–1)

The head's credibility with staff often rests on how well they are perceived to handle such issues, and because there is almost inevitably some difference within staffs about the balance of punishment and welfare, it is also almost inevitable that some will wish the head to do something rather more or less than what they actually did. This difference of opinion is generally – but not always – able to be managed. What is more stressful is when an event escalates or just goes on and on without ever seeming to be resolved.

In addition to the risks attached to just having to work through a disciplinary situation that never seems to get any better, the other major risk for heads and their schools is that events will escape the confines of the school grounds and seep into the community and/or media (see Chapter 6). Community perceptions of schools are distinctive: anything bad seems to have immediate effect, whereas it can take a lot of good things over a long period of time to alter a negative perception. A backfence story about an ongoing discipline problem can soon turn into a neighbourhood myth about a school out of control. Equally as damaging can be the unfortunate story in the local media about a single difficult disciplinary incident which is then taken to be universally true. Some editors, keen for anything that sells, offer money for such stories and/or mobile phone footage. Heads are always grateful when what they know could be turned into an alarming news headline doesn't actually make it into print (see Box 5.10).

Because discipline is part of everyday teaching, many prospective applicants may *not* be put off by having to continue to deal with questions of social order as heads. On the other hand, some may see this as a reason not to bother, since more responsibility for discipline rests with the head. Furthermore, it is the head who has to deal with staff conflicts over discipline, and to answer any troublesome questions from media.

There can be a decided Groundhog Day feeling attached to predictable issues. Having to deal with staffing, building and discipline day after day after day after day can simply just wear some serving heads out.

Supply and predictable risks

In seeking to attract people to headship, there is no point simply focusing on the reasons why the job is worth doing. Predictable issues are largely

---

Box 5.10 Managing the media risk

I eventually put the parent on a kind of contract. She would give me twenty-four hours to resolve the issue and if I hadn't, *then* she could go to the media.

(Secondary head, Australia)

unrecognized in job applications. These do not require vision, creativity, enthusiasm, vitality or drive to resolve. They *do* require energy and stamina and good humour which features in some job advertisements, but also calm, patience, empathy, wisdom and judgment, which generally do not (see Chapter 3). If prospective applicants see that the actual everyday work of headship is sufficiently unattractive, arduous and/or unrecognized and undervalued, then many will make the decision not to do it. School governing bodies that fail to describe accurately the predictable, everyday, 'village jobs' that heads do run the risk of not looking for – and getting – the right person for the job.

For heads themselves, dealing with the predictable carries personal and professional risks. Any aspect of dealing with staffing, buildings or troubled and troublesome families can spiral out of control and end up in litigation or unwanted external attention. Any one issue can drag on for months on end, and become a serious drain on time and effectiveness. In combination, predictable issues can also become the dominant motif of daily educational life. They can also, singly and/or in combination require too much from the head, and send the precarious balance of work, family and leisure out of kilter. I explore this further in the next chapter.

Chapter 6

Heads or tails

The problem of controlling the unpredictable

When children gazed into the large, luminous, sea-green eyes of *The demon headmaster* (Cross, 1982), they were immediately sleepy, then insensible and completely biddable. Seated in the school hall, they were read a litany of facts and figures which they could then regurgitate for any test. The school was orderly and safe, policed by a small number of sadistic, robotic Prefects. This subliminal pedagogy, stupefyingly cheap and effective, was of course a plot to rule the country. The head's evil plan was foiled by a small group of children, some of whom were not amenable to hypnotism, and one of whom, despite being mesmerized, was able to work out what was going on. It was the head's incapacity to conceive of this possibility that led to his demise on national television.

While this imaginative tale of devilish educative efficiency is intended to entertain children, real and aspiring headteachers may notice two things. The first is that while hyper-control is something that many heads occasionally and secretly wish for, it is clearly a fantasy. The second, that no matter how good the plan or the head's skills there are some things which just can't be controlled and/or predicted, is absolutely the reality.

This chapter concerns those things which appear on the local radar too late to be headed off, and which are thus unexpected. It focuses on those things which could happen to anyone at any time, but generally don't. These are things which occur in the public eye, and are the result of serendipity or bad luck, rather than anything else (see Box 6.1). They are serious crises or emergencies of one kind or another.

The Quick Reference Handbook for School Leaders lists a number of types of emergencies that might be faced by schools. These are:

- Accident or fire in the community
- Assault or suspected rape
- Bomb threat
- Building system or mechanical malfunction
- Chemical or other hazardous spill
- Death of a pupil or staff member at school or at home

> **Box 6.1 Blind bad luck**
>
> Heads developed the custom of sending messages, cards and flowers to colleagues who suddenly found themselves the victim of circumstances. We woke up, saw the front page or heard the breakfast news, and thought that could be me, it's only chance thats it's not. We also wanted to offer assistance if any was required. My first experience of this was in the early '80s when the all-white students in our school went 'on strike' because they didn't want a Language Centre for Vietnamese and Cambodian refugees. National media turned up in amazingly short time, followed by the federal Race Relations Commissioner. For a short time we became the crucible in which historical tensions around 'Asia' and Australia's notorious White Australia Policy played out. A decade later, two of my neighbouring colleagues experienced much the same, but with National Action (the Australian version of the National Front) this time leading the charge. In their case, constant harassment via leaflets, posters and the web, and the occasional death threat, made resolution of the immediate issues much more difficult. Everyone knew, in each case, that this kind of incident could have happened to anyone. It was just blind bad luck it occurred where it actually did.
>
> (Researcher journal, 2001)

- Drug overdose, poisoning or allergic reaction
- Field trip incident
- Fire in the school
- Intruder or confrontational person
- Kidnapping, hostage situation, missing child or murder
- Large group disturbance or gang fight
- Severe weather or earthquake
- Shooting or use of other weapon.
  (National Association for Headteachers, 2007, pp. 212–13)

This chapter addresses these kinds of natural disasters and human events. They can sometimes spiral way out of control and end up not only in unwanted public attention but also in serious consequences for most concerned. The chapter does not deal with harm minimization, disaster planning and emergency procedures (see Macneil and Topping, 2007, for a review of 'best practice'). It assumes that heads have these in place, as they are required to do by law. It also assumes that heads understand that they need specific forms of crisis communication with the local education authorities, emergency services and with families. And it assumes that heads are prepared and able to take a positive stance towards the media.

Experienced heads *do* have systems in place to avoid being caught out. A team from the London Institute of Education (Riley *et al.*, 2005), working with heads in a range of inner urban schools, pursued how the heads found out about potential risks within their neighbourhoods. They ascertained that these heads had developed over time a kind of 'mental filter' which they used to determine which events or incidents might result in an undesirable outcome:

> [They] attended to a range of sources within the school and local community … Nothing was ignored (or if it was, participants felt it was at their peril) … They were always on the look out for the signs: body language … informal feedback … the energy and importance they gave to the task of gleaning community knowledge, cultural intelligence, was often a reflection of the fragility of their school contexts: the ease with which things could fall apart … They ignored nothing, as the small and anecdotal rumour … could have as big an impact as a child being excluded from school … listening to the local news on the radio on the way in to school can be an accurate indicator of the difficulties you may face on arrival.
>
> (ibid., pp. 17–18)

Nevertheless, despite even the best intelligence, things happen.

Natural and unnatural disasters

Natural and unnatural disasters place huge pressures on schools, and only some of these are able to be predicted at the last minute. Others take everyone by surprise. Fire, flood and earthquake are not common events yet they occur often enough for them to be significant.

Like headteachers and school staffs, local authorities are generally good at handling any immediate crisis. They send in people to secure buildings and they send in counsellors. They organize temporary accommodation if it's necessary. And colleague heads are also ready to lend a hand. If the buildings are badly damaged, there are ultimately unexpected new replacement facilities generally superior to what was destroyed. In the period between the crisis and this outcome, however, there is time spent in temporary and unsatisfactory accommodation, frustrated teachers, uncomfortable children and disgruntled parents. Heads must manage this period, in which learning and morale can plummet, quietly and generally alone (see Box 6.2).

Floods are often more difficult to cope with than fire. Because fires are mostly deliberately lit, no-one questions whether the school or school buildings should reopen. This is not the case with flooding, where questions may be raised about the suitability and viability of the location. The sheer cost of rebuilding after fire or flood often creates litigious debates between insurers, and levels of government. Media soon see the events as an old story, only amenable to the

Box 6.2 The consequences of fire

At least I didn't get permanent breathing problems like one of my friends who was sent too soon into a building where the noxious fumes hadn't dissipated ... but having one entire ground floor of eight general classrooms out of action for the best part of two years placed a huge strain on routines and patience ... not to mention managing the reconstruction project ... we had to learn new skills in project management in a hurry ... Some children just couldn't forget about their frogs boiling to death, it just came up time and time again ... and the staff struggled to make up for losing a professional lifetime's worth of teaching resources ... I was really really frustrated with the glacial pace at which decisions about funding and the actual renovation were proceeding. In the end, the school had a fantastic renovation with two self-contained pods instead of the eight egg-crate classrooms ... we learnt how to redesign inside an old-fashioned shell ... we then applied this to renovating the other classroom blocks ... Of course, I'd left by then.

(Secondary head, Australia)

occasional whatever-happened-to ... Public interest in the events and their aftermath dwindles, and those who are affected are left, sometimes for years, to put their lives, homes and services back together again. Heads must deal with such consequences.

The aftermath of Hurricane Katrina in New Orleans is a prime example. Most US citizens are aware that the sheer scale of the tragedy combined with the racialized responses of the federal government has meant that areas of the city are still not adequately reconstructed. However, the details of the reality for families trying to put the fabric of their lives back together, including their schools, are often lost. Katrina completely destroyed 110 out of 166 schools in the city alone, and while children were dispersed to other parts of the country to attend schools, many students missed large amounts of schooling. School records were lost and many teachers found jobs elsewhere. Large numbers of students have not returned to the city. As part of its rebuilding programme, the city redesigned its system to operate more like a series of charter schools, and the schools which are being rebuilt are much better designed and equipped than before. However, at the very same time that this innovation was initiated, families were living in temporary toxic trailers.[1] Many of the city's children suffer ongoing trauma. One art therapy programme revealed that hurricane survivor children consistently did not draw houses as a square with a roof – instead they simply drew triangles – roofs. Two years after the events children's drawings were populated by snakes, alligators, dead birds, rescue boats and helicopters.[2] We can only begin to imagine how these human consequences are manifest in the new schools that have been built.

These US hurricanes were of a magnitude that can scarcely be imagined. Disasters of significant proportions also strike in other places, often with less devastation, but also with severely challenging effects for families, neighbourhoods – and students, teachers and heads.

June 2007 was the wettest month on record in the UK. Across the north of the country, in Hull, East Riding, Rotherham and Doncaster, 290 schools were damaged by floods. Some 170,000 children and young people were affected.[3] In Hull, 95 per cent of schools were damaged. The city council claimed that the national government failed to pay the disaster the attention it would if it occurred in a more middle-class locality. Claiming it was a 'forgotten city', the leader of the council said: 'We're having to bus students to other schools. At one school they were finishing their GCSEs ankle deep in water.'[4] Many schools could not open until the start of the new school year in 2007. Even then, for many this meant a Herculean effort (see Box 6.3).

The UK government did fast-track the school building programme for the city allowing the rebuilding of eight schools to be brought forward.[5] However,

---

Box 6.3 Flood damage

Evidence of the deluge is not hard to spot. Discrete piles of ruined computers and other electronic debris dot the site, along with signs of builders working. But head teacher Kevin Beaton says today's school is a world away from the scene of 'total devastation' left by the floods three weeks before the end of the summer term.

'Every single ground floor room was under water to a depth of two or three feet – some had four feet of water. We had 104 classrooms affected as well as the sports hall.' ... the fire brigade pumped out ... 'we moved everything we could save and then we started ripping out the carpets and taking up floors, which had all buckled. In the first week we were on our own really and we had eight or nine members of site staff who worked flat out from six in the morning to nine at night,' said Mr Beaton ... 'You can't panic in these situations – you have got to be calm,' says deputy head Jason Blount. 'This flood was our reality. There was no point crying about it. The important thing was the pupils. You just had to do it' ... Mr Beaton said: 'We have a lot of families still not back in their own houses. A lot of our members of staff not back in their homes. It is really important we open because it relieves some of the pressure from these families' ... ultimately the floods will improve things. 'I think it will be a better school. We have to get to the end of November when all the building work will be finished, – but we will have better facilities in the end.'

(BBC News 4 September 2007, www.news.bbc.co.uk/go/pr/fr/-/1/hi/education/6977819.stm; accessed 27 April 2008)

two special schools remained closed well into the new school year, with pupils dispersed to other sites.[6]

It might well be thought that these are exceptional cases, and they are, although there is widespread agreement that changes in the earth's atmosphere are likely to continue to produce very severe weather. England in particular is expected to have ongoing issues with flooding, even if not on the scale experienced by the north of England in 2007.

Events that have such major repercussions are not so remote that heads do not know that dramatic and critical natural and unnatural disasters are possibilities which are randomly distributed. With luck, most heads and their schools avoid them. The unlucky have no choice not only to manage but also to show a kind of courage and leadership that is rarely recognized and rewarded.

The WOW factor – events With Out Warning

Heads can predict that they will have to deal with human crises. It is not uncommon for heads to have to deal with the effects of a staff member who becomes seriously ill, a child who has an accident or a relatively serious fight between students. While no schools in the West have to have funeral committees, as do many in Africa where the casualties of the AIDS epidemic produce a frighteningly regular need, some schools and heads do have more frequent calls on their capacities to deal with tragedy. Apparently random rural communities are periodically unduly susceptible to youth suicide, poverty-stricken urban suburbs have disproportionate levels of gun and knife crime – and headteachers in such places *must* deal with these events.

And whether life-threatening or not, whether predictable or not, some events are just crises. Local media are heavily implicated in the process of an event becoming critical. Because they are keen to report all events at local schools, local media are literally attuned to service calls to emergency services. Heads often find themselves simultaneously dealing with an actual emergency or crisis and issuing statements to the press and sending letters home to parents. Considerable headteacher effort sits behind what are relatively commonplace kinds of news stories (see Box 6.4). These, however, are precisely the kinds of events which make parents very worried and are likely to produce a continued spate of queries.

Sometimes it is not a single event *per se*, but rather a series of things that become a media crisis (Box 6.5).

Crises can also arise from ongoing interactions with the community and/or from unresolved issues within the school itself. For example, racist incidents have a nasty way of hanging on. They have been on the increase in the post-9/11 world (see Boxes 6.6 and 6.7), and heads often find themselves dealing with community views and beliefs which run counter to discrimination laws. Such views cannot be condoned, but at the same time, those who hold them must be allowed the opportunity to change their behaviour.

Box 6.4 A small incident which might cause ongoing problems

There is no need to increase security at the York primary school where two nine-year-old boys were shot with a pellet gun [said the head] ... police were called to St Lawrence's CE Primary School in Heslington Road, to reports that a youth had fired a pellet gun through the school fence and into the play-ground at about 11.20 am. The two pupils were hit by pellets while playing football and police said they both suffered reddening to an arm.

(York Press, wwwyorkpress.co.uk/misc/artic = 2208907; accessed 19 April 2008)

Box 6.5 A media-manufactured crisis

[T]he investigations [of 11 teachers' sexual abuse of children, 9 of which were unsubstantiated] have had an impact on the school. Television vans were frequently parked at the bottom of the drive and the *Daily Mail* branded it a school for scandal. At the height of the investigation, Steve [the head] spent at least two days a week involved in the inquiry process, helping police, trawling through data or comforting staff, which has slowed down progress at the school. He says: 'We simply haven't had the time to spend on policy devel-opment, self-evaluation and new staffing structures. It's had a big impact on our budget as well.'

(*Times Educational Supplement*, Magazine, 23 March 2007, p. 19)

Contentious community views can also emerge in relation to school policies on gender, exclusion and/or safety. Schools seeking to improve sexual health advice can find themselves at the centre of pro-life protests.[7] Schools simply implementing national science curriculum may find themselves embroiled in power struggles with religious communities with firm counter-views (see Apple, 2001). In cases where there is open confrontation between the school and parents or community members, the head must exercise con-siderable restraint.

Ignoring such incidents and issues does not make them go away and indeed often inflames the situation. However, addressing them can also precipitate further critical events. Heads who take the risk to take on such issues do so with their fingers and toes metaphorically crossed. And any one of these kinds of events can make it into media.

In critical public situations the fragility of the head's position is clear. They must not only make a wise (and sometimes brave) decision in the first

Box 6.6 Handling a difficult issue

[T]here was quite an unpleasant assault by four younger boys on an older boy and the unfortunate thing about it ... it was outside of school and there was an expectation that the school would deal with it, which we did, but the parents of the boy that was assaulted felt that the boys should be excluded – certainly the main instigator, they were all in Year 7 and physically quite little ... the boy that was assaulted wasn't badly hurt to the point where he was hospitalized or anything like that and there were no weapons or anything like that used but the parents wouldn't let it drop. They felt that the boys should have been permanently excluded and I didn't ... for all sorts of reasons. ... he was a looked after child and I didn't think it warranted a permanent exclusion ...

And this just rumbled back and forth and it was kind of like bordering on a racist incident because the four boys who had committed the assault were either black or dual heritage and the boy who was the victim was a white boy. So the parents of the white boy were trying to say it was a racist incident and it exposed quite a lot of racist attitudes on their part which actually was helpful to me because it meant that I could sort of call their bluff basically. But it did go on for quite a while and I had to involve the local authority ...

I had a situation where I had the two parents leafleting my parents on an open evening when their own son – the boy that was the victim – was actually helping out at the open evening. So you had the parents at the gate handing leaflets out to try and prevent parents from choosing the school with some very inflammatory and racist comments on them which I really took them to task over. Inside the school I've got their son helping the department do a presentation for the open evening and I'm really not able to reconcile this. I did try and have a rational conversation with the parents but it just wasn't possible. But I dealt with it and it was resolved and with the best possible outcome because those boys are still in school and there have not been any further incidents and the parents have backed off and the local authority is very pleased with the outcome and the fact that we didn't get into the media and all the rest of it.

But that stuff takes time. I did spend some hours on what I should put in the letter to them and how do I challenge what they are saying but not so much that it makes it aggressive and inflammatory.

So all the time we [heads] are trying to be very deliberate and very careful and mindful of the potential of anything that you say – to students; to staff; to parents. You've got to be a lot more considerate and sometimes you haven't got the time to be as considerate as you might want to be but there is probably more that will come down on you if you don't consider your response.

(Secondary head, UK)

Box 6.7 The loneliness of handling a crisis

[N]obody knew what it was like for a school like ours after 9/11 ... and the worse thing is that nobody wanted to know and that included the director of education. We had no guidance at the time about how to deal with a parent who comes in crying because she's been abused in John Lewis [department store] or a parent who's been spat on in the street. Parents were saying that they felt ashamed to be Muslim – ashamed to be British and Muslim. And they had their own reasons for wanting to talk about it so I phoned the local authority for some guidance and they just said ignore it. But that didn't work ...

But what actually you do get hope from is when the local head from the Islamic school came in and spoke to the staff and children. That's the kind of support you need. I knew it was bad when he walked into his first assembly and he was wearing religious dress and one of the children shouted out 'Jihad'. They were interesting times ... he was talking to a kid who had done a piece of work where he said that he wanted to be a suicide bomber. And that's when you start to think that you've got a real problem ...

I don't think I did know what to do but my solution was that if you don't know what to do, then let's talk about it and let's find out how we can do it because if we don't open it up, we are going to get diversity of opinion and you'll get groups saying different things ... unless you open yourself up, it won't be solved.

So it was just a matter of the fact that this was here and you had kids coming out with the idea that it was God's will. But these are children in our school, for God's sake, and no child is born bad ... what we should be doing in school is talking about it and opening the whole thing up. How do they feel?

And once we'd opened it up with the children and they talked about their family ... and the parents were saying that it wasn't right ... then the children's view wasn't that this was a good thing ...

So, I suppose, that just helped tremendously. I think it strengthened the relationship between the school and the community because the school very much opened itself up to the community.

(Primary head, UK)

instance but then also deal calmly with whatever results, even when it runs very real risks of spiralling out of control – which it sometimes does. The head is not entirely in control of such events. Others in the situation also have agency, and their actions can often make it very difficult to find a resolution.

Schools are not shut off from what happens outside the school gates and they must often work through highly complex and emotive issues. The loneliness of leadership is palpable when heads talk about what this actually means in practice (see Box 6.7).

A key quality required of headteachers in these kinds of crises is the ability to make good decisions. Studies of decision-making in high risk situations suggest that people generally call on similar examples in order to help them decide what to do in new circumstances (Breakwell, 2007). If heads encounter something that is very different from their actual and/or learned experiences, then they may well struggle to know what to do. If time is of the essence, and it often is, then they may find themselves relying more on intuition than on any set of rules (Gilovich *et al*., 2002; Laming, 2004). Studies of headteacher decision-making suggest that they tend to be pragmatic (Strike, 1994), doing what is least harmful, and in crisis situations this may well be what is required. Later, they may revert to more rule-bound or 'moral reasoning' (Strike *et al*., 1998). Evans (1999) argues that heads make decisions pragmatically and that these are not pedagogic. However, in the examples shown here (Boxes 6.6 and 6.7), both heads acted decisively on the basis of deeply held principles of justice.

More dramatic events cause major disruption to schools and have ripple effects throughout the neighbourhood. Dealing with a death in which a school or schools are implicated can make enormous immediate demands. And some heads do have to manage extremely calamitous events. These are inevitably randomly distributed and unpredictable.

Take, for example, the case of the Snowtown murders[8] in South Australia, where, in 1999, the bodies of eight victims were found in plastic barrels in a disused bank vault, and a further two bodies were found buried in a back yard. The schools adjacent to these sites faced an immediate media onslaught (see Box 6.8).

After the first round of sensation, and in the absence of information, print media began to undertake 'in-depth' reports on the locality and to speculate about the causes of the horrific events. Much of this was in the form of highly deficit portraits of a region hard hit by unemployment. This reporting was hard for the schools to deal with: they experienced it as unfair and directly counter to the work they were trying to do. All of them subsequently took a range of actions to promote their schools and the locality. School 2 (in Box 6.8) won a national literacy prize for their efforts to write about the positive aspects of their community.

The potential longer-term effects of the Snowtown trial on families, schools and neighbourhoods were substantially decreased by an unprecedented series of court injunctions, many still in place, which prevent details being made public. Such legal protection does not always happen, and the repercussions of these kinds of horrific events can hang on and on. Columbine, for example, has been subject to an ongoing barrage of attention, much of it self-serving, rather than stories being written with the interests of the families, the school, or the community at the forefront (Watson, 2002).

Heads facing such aftermaths need equal amounts of perceptiveness, tact, diplomacy and persuasion. This may be because

Box 6.8 Dealing with a horrific crisis

The whole day here was awful ... the one day when they found the second body, there were helicopters over here all day, five helicopters, five different ones, they started early and they just circled and circled. Kids, staff, parents, everybody, it took a long time to get them back, to get all of them ... that lasted more than a day.

(Head, School 1)

And we had one family who lived next door, so she was interviewed on TV ... but there were a number of other families too that were opposite the house and digging was until two and three in the morning and ... the school was just hyped up ... with the news helicopter over all the time ... it was constantly around.

(Head, School 2)

When the news came out we had kids out by the fences with the teachers and that was stopped pretty quickly. It's like you don't go out there, this area's out of bounds ... there was an assembly ... a lot of the kids were in shock ... we put stuff in the newsletter ... offered free counselling to kids and families ... During that week there were the gawkers, you know stacks of gawkers lined up ... people out there with their deck chairs ... and even things like lunch vans coming along and you could see them on television, the lunch vans coming along and selling lunches to the gawkers.

(Deputy head, School 3)

We needed to tell children that your next door neighbour isn't a murderer, and there aren't dead bodies in every house next door to you, that this is really unusual.

(Head, School 2)

[T]he kids [of one of those charged] enrolled here were actually gone before the bodies were found ... but there is another family involved where the lady is on our school council ... I haven't spoken to anyone in the school about this and I won't ... the lady hasn't spoken about it ... she's doing the best to get on with her life.

(Head, School 4)

[T]here was one class used it for media studies, they actually went out with a video camera taking shots of all those people sitting there and that was their project for the year ... another class had to do some writing but a student directly involved, her mother was very upset and didn't want it discussed.

(Deputy head, School 3)

[T]raumatised teachers and staff are themselves vulnerable to traumatic reminders of the event such as the school itself, the site of destruction or reconstruction, loud noises, empty desks of injured children. These reminders may increase their own reactions, may increase weak areas, and/or may interfere with their ability to function.

(Nader and Pynoos, 1993)

In the wake of emergencies, there is an increased demand on headteachers to be vigilant for signs that all is not well. This is generally not included in official requirements for disaster and emergency planning which tend to focus only on the immediate. Where counselling is provided, it is most usually in the short term, and any subsequent follow-up intervention may take considerable effort on the part of the headteacher to action. Teachers must be persuaded that they need it, and authorities must be persuaded that it is necessary. At a time when teacher unions are concerned about escalating violence against their members, there may also be considerable pressure in the form of union action for other kinds of action to be taken (see Box 6.9). Heads have to manage and mediate such pressures.

Sometimes crises are manufactured by those who ought to know better. Box 6.10 illustrates an extreme case of contractual negligence. This is an example of a drawn-out crisis. While problems with buildings are routine and they sometimes produce ongoing difficulties, it *is* rare to find an example like the one below. However, smaller versions of this incident are not uncommon.

Box 6.9 Pressure to take action over pupil behaviour

Caretakers, technicians and secretaries have voted to back teachers refusing to accept the return of two pupils who threatened to kill their PE master. Members of the GMB, the union for production and service workers, voted to take industrial action which could close Glyn Technology School in Ewell, Surrey. The boys, aged 15 and 16, were expelled over their hate campaign which included 44 death threats but they were then reinstated by an independent appeal panel. Teachers belonging to the Association of Teachers and Lecturers voted last week to refuse to have them in their classes and the other two teacher unions are expected to back the stance next week. Surrey County Council said one family had agreed that their son should attend a different school but the other parents wanted reinstatement. In the meantime, they are receiving home tuition.

(www.telegraph.co.uk/news/main.jhtml?xml = /news/2002/10/17/nbul17.
xml#4; accessed 4 November 2007)

Box 6.10 The crisis of shoddy building work

Giles Brook School headteacher Philip Scull has been 'totally vindicated' over his stand on building problems that saw the flagship but fault-ridden school closed. Cllr Andy Dransfield, chairman of Milton Keynes Council's Audit Committee made the dramatic concession at a re-convened special hearing into what went wrong ...

The Committee heard from MP Dr Phyllis Starkey who was called in by Mr Scull almost as the school was opened in 2004. She saw faults ... which she passed on to council chief executive ... By October 2006 Dr Starkey said she was in almost daily contact with Giles Brook and that in November called for an Independent Inquiry ... in December her notes recalled: 'a bit of ceiling fell down just after my visit'. Giles Brook was eventually closed down amid concerns roof beams could collapse and rebuilding work continues there ...

Then it was the turn of Mr Scull who told councillors even on its opening day Giles Brook looked just like a building site. 'You did not need to be an expert to see the problems. The bricklaying was indescribable, there were gaps in the timber cladding – we had two rat and mice infestations in the first year ... we thought Building Control would not have allowed it.' The problems placed huge stress on staff, children and parents. He said they had lost five years of the school's life. 'We hope to be back at the end of this term – and then we will have to start all over again,' he said.

(*Milton Keynes Citizen*, 4 February 2008; www.miltonkeynes.co.uk/news/Giles-Brook-school-headteacher-39totally.3742411.jp; accessed 19 April 2008)

It is salutary to think about how much time this head spent on trying to get the problems with his new build taken seriously, how much he must have worried about the safety of staff and students, and how much time this took away from the other tasks he was meant to do.

Sometimes heads themselves are at the epicentre of the crisis. Like teachers, they are vulnerable to those who would deliberately make mischief for them (see Box 6.11).

In dealing with large numbers of competing demands and numerous issues and events, any one of which could transmogrify into a crisis but generally don't, heads daily flirt with potential crises. Most heads can *readily* imagine themselves as:

- the head of the school in Soham who trusted the judgement of police that the new caretaker was reliable and no danger to children;[9]
- the head of the New Zealand school where six students and a teacher died in a white water rafting accident;[10]

Box 6.11 False accusations

[A] girl accused me of hitting her. Apparently I was with another member of staff and there were a load of kids there and it was a family that have a history of seeking compensation from public bodies. She was trying to lead a school strike and she was positioning herself on the playground and trying to get children to take part. So I went out and she wouldn't look at me to talk so I put my hand on her arm and I said: 'Look at me' and then she did and she accused me of grabbing her by her shoulders and squeezing so hard that she was bruised. So she then went to the police but she wouldn't allow the injury to be photographed but she gave evidence. The police rang me up and said that they wanted to talk to me so I invited them in but they said I had to report to the police station with a solicitor.

So I had to go in and I was put in a cell ... I was stunned because I didn't expect that and, for a while, I didn't know what was happening. They read me my rights and I was interviewed under caution and the police said to me afterwards that she was wasting our time but because the family were so persistent the police decided to take further action. Eventually it was resolved but the family still go round the city saying that I hit their child. And obviously she was supposed to be at the school so we had to work out how to resolve that and, again, that dragged on for six months and for a few weeks I didn't know if I was going to be suspended and there was a meeting called ... all that goes on in the background.

(Secondary head, UK)

'Mrs Smith accuses you of assaulting her son – contacting the police.' The message came towards the end of an all-day video conference with the National College for School Leadership, reports Ray Tarleton. Discussion on how strong school leaders might help weaker ones suddenly took on a new meaning.

At lunchtime, I had supported the duty team, tidying the queue and checking litter. I came across a large group in the sports hall foyer being pushed into a small space under the stairs. I restrained the ringleader from behind just as he was about to make another lunge. An enraged parent might just believe the story of a head grabbing their child and leaving bruise marks on his arm. The fact that her son had previously been excluded three times for violent assaults and had been involved with the police because of violence outside school meant that she knew her rights. The unexpected visit from the chair of governors that night alerted me to the potential seriousness of the situation. As we trotted over to the sports hall to check the CCTV footage, I realised I was now an alleged aggressor rather than the rule of law. As I was the main suspect, the police investigation had to be done without me. The child protection panel issued its usual demands for the head's suspension. My chair of governors bravely refused.

> While the head feels he is no longer in control and at the mercy of others' decisions, the process can destabilise governors. At a time when they wished to lend support and needed to be informed about what was happening, in order to reassure the community, the lights were switched off. They were plunged into darkness.
>
> The allegation was a topic of conversation among students and parents, yet the rules prevented governors from knowing what was going on. As governors would hear the case, they had to be untainted, free from any knowledge of the event for the possible disciplinary panels. A letter to them warned of certain unspecified allegations against the head. They were not to ask questions or try to discuss the matter. Their imaginations were racing. What had the head done? Fingers in the till? Internet porn? The process dragged on for weeks. Two of my assistant heads rallied magnificently, organising the investigation. The police interviewed more than 60 witnesses. The time and labour involved were staggering.
>
> (*TES*, 5 January 2007; www.tes.co.uk/2335361; accessed 6 December 2007)

- the head of one of the 19 US schools where, in the 2007–8 school year, students attacked their peers with guns;[11] or
- the head of the South Australian school where the local Opposition Party hoped to whip up a school safety crisis on the back of a relatively trivial knife incident.[12]

Sleepless nights are spent pondering whether there were clues that would have predicted what might happen. Could these have been acted on even if they had been spotted? Would concerns for natural justice and proof have prevented any action being taken anyway? Such is the stuff of headteacher nightmares.

In all crisis situations, no matter how large or small, horrific or tragic, in the media or out of it, heads must do what is required at the time. They must then cope with the aftermath and if necessary must manage whatever media chooses to do with the events. They must often work politically to ensure that issues are resolved. In all of these cases, they have to dig deep to handle the residual guilt that inevitably accompanies crises and emergencies.

If only they had known ... if only they had done ...

Developing a tolerance for crises?

Readers may think that I have cited isolated examples in this chapter. There is almost no systematic research into the kinds of incidents I have been describing here, and there ought to be. We just don't know how many heads have to deal with these kinds of incidents, how often, and how many some have to face at once. I had quite a lot of examples to choose from in my own research and experience and from media reports.[13] My belief is that rather more heads than might be commonly believed do have eventful careers.[14] By the time fires, serious fights, deaths of students on school trips, litigation, media exposure and drawn-out disputes are put together, there is an important minority picture of the random distribution of crises. This is a geography of heads and schools put under pressure.

Ray Tarleton (the head who appears in Box 6.11) is quite public about what he has had to deal with (see Box 6.12). He speaks of his experiences in order to assist new and aspiring heads to understand what they may face, and perhaps also to assure his colleagues that they are not alone in dealing with problems that stretch their capacities. Of course, a lifetime crisis list may or may not be reassuring to new and aspiring heads and Tarleton runs a risk of scaring as many as he prepares. Nevertheless, I am clearly with him, as this chapter attests, in arguing that the management of crises, and their dimensions and demands, must be made public rather than being kept quiet.

Emergencies, crises and critical incidents put heads to the test. The primary risk is not the time it takes to manage them, as is the case with the predictable risks discussed in Chapter 5. Rather it is in the lack of control that the head has about how events might proceed. Crises demand a necessary reactivity, an inevitable reliance on the good judgement and ethical behaviour of others. Heads need to be able to handle the stress that arises when management actions are undertaken in conditions of actual or potential intense scrutiny, external judgment and litigation.

English headteacher Mike Mander[15] has been studying how heads deal with critical incidents and he argues that heads who are able to deal with incidents singly often feel beleaguered when they erupt in rapid succession – which they sometimes do. His recommendations include developing an open, no blame, staff culture where incidents are regularly and routinely discussed.

Box 6.12 Not one incident but many

There have been other pressure points in my 19 years as a head: a gas leak that resulted in a full-scale school evacuation; a knifing incident in the town with police helicopters and areas cordoned off; bomb alerts and even a telephone message from an irate parent who told me he had a gun and would be in the school in 20 minutes (he later handed himself over to police). In all these cases, the first resource is common sense, calm reflection, good humour and a reliance on the collective judgement of your team.

(Tarleton, 2008, p. 27)

Following his argument, crises can be seen as best not managed by charismatic, visionary, entrepreneurial and creative heads, however desirable those qualities might be. In emergencies what is needed are heads with large emotional reserves, the capacity to think quickly and wisely, the courage to trust their own judgement, and the ability to talk to an enormous variety of people, some of whom are not necessarily reasonable or calm. These qualities are generally not specified in current English job advertisements (Chapter 3). And not all teachers believe they are up to this kind of challenge and not all serving heads wish to be in a situation where they have to do so.

To make matters even more complicated, the repercussions of failing to control the unpredictable and/or failing to make the consequences of unpredictable crises disappear can, as heads in this and the previous chapter have suggested, rebound badly in student alienation and poor results, And this can have very serious consequences for heads and schools, as the next chapter shows.

Chapter 7

Off with their heads

The problem of new accountabilities

'Failing schools' are the bane of government policy-makers. Most nations, rich and poor, have shifted the way they approach attaining a more equitable distribution of educational 'goods' and have adopted variations of 'quality management'. These generally include some form of national benchmarking for student achievement via the use of indicators, tests and/or standards which are applied to all schools and all children. Systemic 'performance' is regularly measured using either a sample or census battery of tests to 'show' the gap between the top and the bottom and what change has occurred over time. Such data may also allow areas and localities 'performing below' the standard to be identified. As both a product and a producer of this shift in accountability policy and practice, nations themselves are subject to global comparisons to show which is 'doing better' (e.g. Angus, 2004; Ball, 1998; Burbules and Torres, 2000; Dale, 1999; Lawn and Lingard, 2001; Taylor *et al.*, 1997).

In some countries, policy-makers have adopted a 'get tough' approach to school failure. The persistent nexus between poverty, levels of family education and poor schooling outcomes are sheeted home to patchy teaching and to some inadequate, ineffective schools. Efforts to improve the system are made through a combination of the following measures:

- consumer choice and competition – believed to produce more effective and efficient performance;
- subsidiarity – it is believed that best performance occurs when local providers tailor services to local conditions;
- identification of high performers – best practice is believed to be transferable;
- identification of poor performers – it is believed that a mix of pressure and support will make them 'lift their game'. Failure to comply can result in termination/closure.

Each of these policy beliefs is contested and there are conflicting views about whether these measures do what they claim (Ball, 2007; e.g. Bowe *et al.*,

1992; Chitty, 1997; Codd, 2005; Gewirtz, 2002; Hood, 1998; Lauder *et al.*, 1999; Marginson, 1997; Thomson, 1998; Whitty *et al.*, 1998).

The changes addressed in this chapter focus on the effects of the new forms of 'accountability' which are embedded in this policy régime.

A note on accountability

To be accountable is simply to have to account to somebody for what has been done. Some decades ago, teachers' public accountability to the wider community was for a social task, to educate children and young people to be citizens, family and community members and productive workers. Schools and teachers judged their actions by how well they did this and they reported to their local school community. They also had to meet whatever requirements were transmitted via local or central policies – these were generally few in number.

More recent accountability policies and institutional arrangements (explained further through the case study in this chapter) have a narrower focus and use quantifiable outputs and outcomes derived from centralized standards/standardized procedures/targets. Data from schools are intended not only to improve systemic and individual practice, but also to demonstrate locally, nationally and internationally that a good job has been done. Demonstration requires the use of practices of continual monitoring.

Critics of these kinds of accountability systems argue that they are unhelpful, morally dubious, and are impractical – too time-consuming, too paper-driven and too inflexible and prescriptive. When applied to schooling, there are toxic side effects (Gillbourn and Youdell, 2000; Gleeson and Husbands, 2001; Gunter, 1997; Mahony and Hextall, 2000; Thomson, 2002; Thrupp, 1999):

- teachers teach to the test;
- schools operate whatever 'triage system' they can think of in order to avoid failure;
- choice is only available to some and not others;
- the very 'disadvantaged' students who are meant to be helped by the system find it alienating and continue to fail;
- measures of improvement are unrealistic;
- they close down professional judgements and the capacity to innovate (see Banks 2004; Bottery, 2000).

Others argue this is not the case (Matthews and Sammons, 2004) and/or that it is possible to bring professional judgement to bear at the same time as the new accountabilities are in place (Banks, 2004).

The remainder of this chapter explores these arguments. It looks at England, arguably the most extreme example of the working out of this approach to quality management. No other country in the world has approached the question of systemic improvement with quite the same zeal and with quite the same effect – although there are near equivalents in some US states.

The English case

It is not possible here to detail all of the changes that have occurred in the past three decades of English education policy (but see Ball, 2008; Jones, 2003; Tomlinson, 2001; Whitty, 2002).

During the 1980s and leading up to the 1988 Education Act (see also Chapter 4) the Conservative government established the framework for:

* parents to exercise some preference for schools;
* devolution of school staffing and budget;
* National Curriculum and testing at Key Stages of schooling;
* local authorities who moved from policy formulation and the provision of school services to a focus on implementation of policy;
* consolidation of moves to more standardized forms of more school-based teacher education.

This was both a re- and de-centralization, with many of the functions which had previously been devolved (curriculum development, for example) now centralized, and those which were formerly regionalized and centralized (staffing, budgets, maintenance) now the responsibility of schools.

In the 1990s, marketized practices of naming and shaming schools via league tables were introduced, together with the notion that headteachers were a key to school improvement. The inspectorate shifted from a formative to a summative function. By the mid-1990s, the category of 'failing schools' and an accompanying set of hefty carrot and stick measures were introduced to 'unstick' them, often with contested results (see the story of Hackney Downs in O'Connor et al., 1999).

The Blair government, elected in 1997, brought in a series of policy adjustments, driven by dismay at the continuing failure of children from the working-class communities that had brought them to power. New Labour made an electoral commitment to raising the base level of educational attainment and immediately focused on systemic measures that they believed might achieve this:

* greater standardization of approaches to the teaching of basic skills through modifications to the National Curriculum, the introduction of national literacy and numeracy strategies – and the ubiquitous four-part whole-class lesson;
* greater standardization of teacher education and of leadership and man-agement of schools;

- improved salary for teachers and introduction of a wider variety of support staff;
- an ambitious school re-building programme;
- more intensive support for those schools with concentrations of 'under-achieving' children via area-based strategies for improvement in high poverty locations (Rees *et al.*, 2007; Thomson, 2008b), now largely replaced by early intervention and interagency approaches;
- introduction of more specialist schools and more lately academies;
- strong rhetorical commitment to creativity and more bespoke curriculum provision together with 'personalization'.

These were not, of course, the entire policy agenda. One of the hallmarks of New Labour has been a kind of 'policy ADHD' in which policy after policy emerged to impact on what policy-makers took to be unacceptably slow change. The other hallmark is its commitment to use centralized regulation and 'test bed pilot schemes' to end what are seen as 'failing schools' (see Harris *et al.*, 2006; Macbeath *et al.*, 2007). This relied on evolving new technologies of accountability.

Accountability system Mark I

The Conservative government replaced the long-standing HMI in 1992 with a new body, OfSTED, whose role was less supportive and more evaluative. The public actions of the first Chief Inspector Chris Woodhead, a strong critic of schools and teachers, were newsworthy but highly inflammatory and he created strong professional opposition. By the turn of the century teacher unions and critics had become more vocal about the practices of naming and shaming, the importation of 'super-heads' into allegedly 'failing schools' (Harris and Chapman, 2002) and the demonstrably inconsistent judgements made by inspection teams (Fidler *et al.*, 1998; Jones and Sinkinson, 2000; Penn, 2002). The National Union of Teachers commissioned a study which advocated school self-evaluation, rather than external inspection, as a more meaningful, relevant and effective means of improvement at both local and systemic levels (Macbeath, 1999; and also then Macbeath, 2000; Macbeath *et al.*, 2000; Macbeath and Sugimine, 2002).

However, this form of inspection did not necessarily result in the kinds of improvement required by government. While schools who were already geared up for improvement found the week-long inspection team either supportive of what they already knew, or even helpful (Cullingford, 1999; Earley, 1998) and at least some of the 'failing schools' (in special measures) did improve enough to be removed from the category (Matthews and Sammons, 2005), some didn't. What's more, there was evidence of some immediate nega-tive post-inspection improvement effects (Rosenthal, 2004) and those schools only marginally better than 'failing' (in serious weaknesses) did not seem to shift (Chapman, 2002; Matthews and Sammons, 2005). There also seemed to be a 'wearing off' of the inspection effects (Perryman, 2005). In addition, it seemed increasingly likely that relatively few teachers actually changed what they were doing after having been judged 'unsatisfactory'. There was also evidence that teacher morale and professional identity were adversely affected by inspection (Case *et al*., 2000; Jeffrey and Woods, 1998) and that only in the highest and lowest performing schools was there evidence of a slight improvement in student exam results (Shaw *et al*., 2003). Another important factor was the sheer expense of these inspection processes.

While policy-makers could and did argue that the first few years of this strategy were successful, test results, the base level measure of systemic improvement, began to bottom out (Fullan, 2006). The equity, effectiveness and efficiency of inspection, as it was, became increasingly questionable.

Accountability system Mark 2

In 2004, the Blair government shifted from a system of external inspection to a new 'light touch system' which used self-evaluation. Media headlines attest to the struggles that led up to this shift – 'Raising standards impossible in some schools' (*Education Guardian*, 5 February 2003); 'Clarke to take out bad headteachers' (*Guardian*, 4 April 2003); 'Retreat over threat to close schools' (*Education Guardian*, 18 August 2003).

The new system required all schools to maintain a continued web-based profile, the Self Evaluation Framework, or SEF. Raw test data were supplemented by a contentious system of 'value added' scores. Inspections were to be more frequent, and schools were to be notified of an inspection two to five days in advance, at which time their SEF would be 'frozen' so that it could not be altered. This move suggested that policy-makers suspected that some schools had managed to 'cheat' the previous system.

The SEF was much more in-line with standards-based manufacturing quality systems which focus not only on outcomes but also on the ongoing processes used to ensure/assure them. Its intent was to moderate the capacity of the school to judge and improve itself. The new system had fewer inspections of actual lessons, and was largely based on school paperwork documenting local quality systems, namely, performance management of teachers, the use of data to diagnose weaknesses, and the development of policy-approved and realistic strategies for improvement. The new 'light touch' inspections relied heavily on test data as the sole measure of quality/standards. Each school was also to have a School Improvement Partner to help in the design and implementation of the quality process (see Box 7.1)

Emerging evidence suggests that this new 'light touch' system is hugely demanding of headteacher time. It produces much more intense and continuous pressure on all schools and teachers to 'perform' (Hall and Noyes, 2008; 2008 in press, see also Box 7.1) – but this may in the long-term prove

Box 7.1 Data-driven improvement

I accompanied my contact on a routine monitoring visit to a cluster of schools that had been working with a consultant over the last two terms. There were two or three middle managers from five schools. They were all young and inexperienced teachers at middle management level. The crisis in recruitment of teachers, coupled with the practice of removing incompetent or unco-operative teachers from schools in Special Measures, means that there are many young and relatively inexperienced teachers at middle management level in difficult schools. The focus of the work was Middle Manager Training. The consultant had facilitated a school-level project with information and advice. On that day the school groups were making presentations to each other about their project. This was the last time the teachers would come together. The Standards and Effectiveness Unit had funded the consultant and the supply cover for the teachers, four days per teacher.

Almost all of the projects concentrated on building data-bases of pupils' prior performances. None of the projects appeared to be training. Clearly the participants had learnt about the value of prior performance data, but the actual project did not seem to take their understanding any further. They spent a lot of time inputting data.

The data handling project appeared to be a proxy for other issues, mostly to do with performance management. For instance, I asked a young and very enthusiastic head of English how her work on comparing English assessment against SAT results would change practice in her classroom. She replied that she wanted to use the information to demonstrate to a more senior colleague that the latter's classes were not progressing as they should. She wanted to highlight the fact that this colleague should do the things that the head of English wanted her to do, such as follow the scheme of work, plan lessons carefully, etc. She explained that this colleague was an important barrier to her department improving its standards in English. Yet she had spent the best part of two terms setting up a data-base and inputting data. In one way or another, all of the participating teachers hoped to use the data to bring less competent teachers into line.

(Alder, 2007, pp. 146–7)

counter-productive. John Macbeath (2006a) has suggested that there is a difference between self-inspection and self-evaluation, and has continued to argue for something other than the current OfSTED régime. School Improvement Partners have also been critiqued as being far removed from the 'critical friends' advocated in self-evaluation texts (Swaffield and Macbeath, 2005). Nevertheless, from a contemporary policy-maker's point of view, light touch inspections address many of the weaknesses in the previous system.

At a systemic level the approach to the diagnosis of systemic weakness also shifted. It too became more consciously 'data-driven'. Targets for school test results, differentiated by socio-economic status (the value-added component) were used to pinpoint those schools who were perceived not to be 'failing', but needing to do better. A new 'category' of school was initiated, schools on 'a notice to improve'. Schools on notice were to be supported and pressured to achieve higher results on tests and exams or else face potential federation, amalgamation or closure. In June 2008, the 638 secondary schools at the bottom of GCSE results tables were named, and brought into a 'National Challenge' scheme aimed at lifting their results. Media coverage focused on the consequences of failure – potential closure or amalgamation – although there was also the promise of some additional funding.[1]

Critiques of the 'blame and big stick approach' – that it is not conducive to organizational learning, that it derives from systemic failure to recognize and address problems early on, that it produces 'quick fix' solutions that fall apart after a short time, that it reinforces the gap between rich and poor schools rather than closes it, that closing schools has devastating effects on communities (Fink, 1999; Hargreaves, 2004; M. Johnson, 1999; O'Connor et al., 1999; Tosey and Nicholls, 1999) – were not taken up. These remain as officially unrecognized concerns about the new, as well as the old, accountability technologies.

Also inherent to both New Labour versions of accountability is an 'ideal headteacher' who turns around a failing/coasting school.

The fictional hero head: Ian George

The 1990s television series *Hope and Glory* featured Hope Park, an English inner-city school in 'special measures', the stage before being declared a complete failure. At the start of the series, Hope Park's vituperative and burnt-out principal was sacked, and a demoralised teaching staff put on notice. Viewers were then introduced to 'super-head' Ian George, played by a smirking Lenny Henry, best known as a stand-up comedian.

George, the publicly fêted head of a 'successful school', was simultaneously head-hunted by Central Office for a highly paid, high-profile consultancy position and by the chair of Hope Park school governors. But George was 'called' to be head teacher of the 'failing school' by his moral outrage at the disrespect shown to students by some staff and the casual curtailment of their education (the students' best hope for a better future), epitomized by the abandoned, vandalized sixth form room. Henry's blackness, bulk and relative youth are used to 'show' that Ian George was an exceptional educator who, in being not white, old and out-of-touch like his predecessor, already had bonds with the local school community and the students. Here, viewers are to understand, was a man with a mission, if not yet a mission statement.

The second episode was set in the holiday period with George preparing for his first school term. The dramatic dilemma was whether he would succeed or fail in his inaugural attempts to make a difference. The action centred on George's efforts to repaint and re-equip the school. As devolved site manager, he had to struggle for additional funds from the local authority to pay for new desks and chairs, while trying to find a local contractor able to deliver on time. George and a team of re-inspired parent and teacher volunteers spent much of their holidays working unpaid with the struggling small furniture business that won the contract they could not possibly meet. They hammered and glued and screwed well into the night before the first day of term. As the (rather too compliant and well-dressed) pupils returned to school, they saw the outside and inside of the school buildings newly painted, the previous terms' damage repaired and graffiti removed. The new furniture was delivered during the first morning assembly, just in (the nick of) time. George's gamble is seen to have paid off, his credibility as new headteacher ushering in new times is symbolically and materially affirmed.

Following episodes showed George getting Hope Park in order – monitoring behaviour in the yard, on the stairs and in the corridors; ensuring that attendance at lessons is checked and followed up; building a new school resource centre; re-establishing the sixth form room and programme; developing systems of and occasions for communication with families; selecting teachers for acting positions in the school management team; and dealing with an incompetent teacher as well as the inevitable episodes of student misbehaviour. He was rarely seen in a classroom or engaged in a curriculum discussion. George *was* frequently shown playing basketball with students in and out of lessons and talking with them in a variety of disciplinary, counselling and informal settings. The audience is given to understand that he is skilled in the craft of teaching, genuine in his commitment and well liked by those who he cares most about – the students.

George's work-load was shown to be enormous. He spent much of the day and night at school. His personal life was disastrous, because the school took priority over all else. When he foolishly initiated a secret sexual relationship with the attractive acting deputy head, it led almost inevitably to her, not his, resignation. The audience, unlike the school staff and students, is privy to George's frequent visits to the doctor and his dismissive attitude towards a potentially troublesome heart condition. In a predictably theatrical series climax, set on the last day of his second term at the school, he put the welfare of the school before his own happiness and well-being for the last time. True to the melodramatic imagination inherent to 'soaps' (Ang, 1985) George was literally driven to death by his determination to succeed on the same glory day that the school received its official reprieve from 'special measures'.

Hope and Glory is a redemption narrative in which a saviour head sacrificed everything for the school and the students. The series takes for granted the idea that the previous 'failure' of the school was directly attributable to the former head. The narrative also 'shows' that inspection and pressure can produce the desired results if everyone tries hard enough – they just have to lift their game and perform as they are meant to.

This is the fiction which guided New Labour and which they have attempted to make reality. Just like Dumbledore (Chapter 3), Ian George is charismatic and heroic. But just like the job advertisements analysed earlier (Chapter 3), New Labour want not only this kind of remarkable hero, but a managerialist Umbridge as well.

Headship as an extreme sport

Headteachers whose schools 'perform' get increased financial rewards (Teacher Support Network, 2006, p. 14). Those who deliver the reality of the fictional 'hero head' get fêted and well publicized and their example is meant to inspire others.

Media stories attest to the difficulties inherent in this kind of régime: 'Heads bullied to boost results, claims union' (*Nottingham Post*, 22 June 2006, p. 1); 'School says truant figures out of date' (*Nottingham Post*, 23 March 2007, p. 7). 'Eton and St Paul's heads boycott independent school's league tables' (*Guardian*). They also attest to some of its casualties.

In February 2008, the *Times Educational Supplement* (8 February 2008, p. 3) carried a story headed 'Inspiring head quits after MP's onslaught'. The article concerned the sudden resignation of the headteacher of a school in an impoverished former mining village. An instant inspection of the school had been triggered by questions asked in Parliament by the local Labour back-bencher. The head's resignation was a response to the anticipated OfSTED report, which was expected to say that the school had not 'sufficiently' improved. The local newspaper (*Worksop Guardian*, 25 January 2008, p. 23) wrote that the school's results had been around 13 per cent level five literacy and 15 per cent level five numeracy in 2001, had been fourth lowest in the national league tables in 2005, but were expected in 2008 to reach targets of 65 per cent in reading and numeracy, but not writing. The *TES* notes that the head's work had been praised by the National College for School Leadership, and that he enjoyed almost total support from the parent community. The local member told the *TES* that the school needed either a new head, new governors, maybe more funding, or perhaps all three. The National Association of Headteachers' general secretary, Mick Brookes, is quoted as commenting: 'You are only as good as your last set of results, like a football manager … This guy should be nominated for an award, not driven out of town.' On the head's resignation, the local authority appointed a neighbouring head to become executive head, prior to it being amalgamated or federated with his school.

This is not a one-off example. Across the country, heads who choose to take the challenge of a 'failing' school are under increasing pressure. Unlike the fictional Ian George who was subject to an inspection which focused on lesson observation, student behaviour and school ethos, life under 'light touch' inspection and the setting of ambitious targets is much more data-driven, risky and pressured.

Media stories hint that for some there is a heavy personal cost from the new accountabilities – 'Inspection pressure drives teachers to suicide' (*The Daily Telegraph*, 11 April 2007). On 12 July 2007, *The Daily Telegraph*[2] reported that a stressed headteacher from Peterborough was 'believed to have committed suicide on the eve of an inspection'. The subsequent Coroner's report confirmed this view. While these clearly are extreme cases, they *are* symptomatic of wider pressures.

The reality is that while many heads grit their teeth and cope with the new accountabilities, some choose to go, and some go because they have no choice but to do so. The remainder of the chapter tells the story of three such heads.

Dave's story: battling on

Dave[3] is head of a large secondary school which serves a former steel-working council estate. He is in his sixth year of headship and has had over the past few years a relatively torrid time. His school is on a 'notice to improve'. The local authority is under a great deal of pressure to make sure that the school improves because it too is on the cusp of being declared a failure because it cannot get its schools to improve quickly enough.

> There's been a change in the local authority because it's one of the core cities and it's under pressure in terms of performance. The DfES says that it is an innovative city and it has lots of initiatives but the impact on achievement has not been what they would want. It has taken the city some time to come to grips with what that means and why, but recently it's just all target performance-based. At the moment the emphasis is very much on results and attainments and what makes the difference there. So they want you to identify who your failing teachers are and sack them. It's all very crude. It's not done from a staff development point of view, it's done from a failure point of view.

Like most heads, Dave was initially optimistic about the shift from inspection to self-evaluation. He assumed that it would mean an end to the pressures to change in ways someone else thought was appropriate. He assumed that judgements would be based on his and his team's analysis of what needed to happen.

> I thought the new self-evaluation framework would help schools in the sense that it would be based on what we were doing but actually they [OfSTED] came in and made judgements. They saw limited things for a day and a half ... it's all on your results and if your results are high enough, you'll get what you want.

In reality, the school's light touch inspection was two days of extreme anxiety:

> On the first morning, one of the inspectors arrived early before the lead
> inspector and his first words were: 'I can't see how you can expect not to
> fail.' In retrospect, I should have done something about that but we
> were focused on what we needed to do just to survive … after the first
> day they provide feedback and they went through the different standards
> and the lead inspector refused to give a grade on leadership and man-
> agement at that point. The whole issue about the difference between
> 'serious weaknesses' and 'notice to improve' is about the capacity of the
> leadership. I thought that they were looking to completely fail us. I
> think they were really gunning for me personally on the second day. He
> told me, on the second day, that he didn't think I was up to the job.

Dave does not object to the idea of ambitions or even some targets, provided
they are realistic and achievable:

> The OfSTED criteria and the whole target-driven thing for schools in
> our sort of position is so tough. I had the behaviour and attendance
> regional advisor in the other day and you know the stuff around persis-
> tent absence? Well, previously it's been 10 per cent but they've reduced
> it now to 9 per cent so all schools are now 9 per cent. But 9 per cent for
> us is different from 9 per cent to a school in a leafy suburb and if the
> government just keeps bringing in arbitrary targets, they are going to
> make our life impossible. The behaviour one is really at odds with the
> inclusion agenda. In this school we've got a large number of kids who
> have all sorts of problems and issues and it does mean that sometimes
> they will sit with their bag on the floor and the lesson will carry on and
> then they'll come back into the lesson. Now that, for me, is good
> teaching but an OfSTED inspector could turn around and say that was
> poor teaching and fail the lesson. So the criterion is that behaviour is
> good if the students actively contribute to the quality of the lesson and
> 'satisfactory' if students merely engage in the lesson. So I'm thinking:
> how are they training them to differentiate between the two? I've got a
> Year 7 at the moment and his reading age is barely on the scale at four
> and he's incredibly immature and he's just running around at the
> moment and we are trying to make sure that he is safe. On an OfSTED
> day, I'd just have to have him out. The last time I actually did some
> teaching I taught this very difficult kid who is in Year 11 now and I
> was observed while I was teaching him. He sat at the back and he joined
> in a bit but he was calm and he was engaged in his own way but it
> would be a negative outcome. I'm not quite sure how OfSTED under-
> stand how we can work. Which is not to say that we shouldn't have
> high aspirations and we don't need to challenge our more able children.

But the alternative is to put these kids out of school somewhere and that's not acceptable to me.

Despite being told by the lead inspector that he was 'too nice' for the job, Dave and the school escaped being put into 'serious weaknesses'. This would have brought significantly greater pressure and the very real risk that not only would Dave lose his job, but also that the school might close.

Dave understands that the system of quality improvement is intended to bring about much needed change for the students that he serves, but he believes that it is a policy developed in the abstract, far away from the actual realities of schools like his. His beliefs are confirmed by the example of a former Blair government speech-writer (Hyman, 2005) who has gone public with his story of the ways in which his view of schools, education policies and teachers were changed by a year working as a teaching assistant in the kind of inner-city comprehensive that his line-manager, Alistair Campbell, famously dubbed 'bog-standard'.

Dave is aware that heads are not the only leaders who risk being sacked if they do not meet expectations, no matter how ambitious:

> Leadership as a head is such a personalized thing. People who are managing directors of firms are not public figures in the same way that a head is. But a head, within your own community, is well known and if you get into trouble, it's front-page news; if a managing director gets paid off or quits, then it might make a few lines in the business page but it's not really news. I wonder whether it is the fact that you are not faceless in the way that a business leader might be?

Public humiliation is one of the risks attached to the new accountabilities. It is a constant risk in Dave's school, and others like it. It is a risk that Dave is still willing to take. The school raised its test and exam scores enough to get out of the 'notice to improve' category. However, Dave's school is now one of the 638 that are 'under-performing' and the pressure on him continues. But, providing he is not debilitated by serious and/or unanticipated crises, Dave seems likely to stay for some time. For him, the job still has enough rewards, satisfaction and joy to make it worthwhile.

John Illingworth's story: retired sick

On 6 June 2006, the BBC's John Humphrys interviewed John Illingworth, a Nottingham (UK) primary headteacher and former president of the National Union of Teachers. The interview[4] was a follow-up to a widely reported speech Illingworth made to the annual NUT conference, where he talked about the overwhelming levels of stress he had experienced as a head, his mental illness and subsequent resignation from headship and from teaching.

In interview, Illingworth suggested that when he first went into teaching he had relative autonomy. This produced good results for children if the teacher was 'good' because there was flexibility to alter the structure of the day and the curriculum to follow particular lines of inquiry:

> I can remember taking children to the local pond on a Monday morning with a few buckets and bringing back buckets of pond water and all the life that was in them and spending a whole week on a little project about what was going on in this pond. We did maths; we did poetry; we did science, obviously. The children loved it. It was a fantastic kind of week spent just centred round what we'd seen in this little pond. You couldn't do that now. Absolutely no way that could be done.

The problem, according to Illingworth, is that subsequent policy interventions intended to alleviate 'patchiness' in teaching quality have strait-jacketed teachers and schools. 'Ridiculous bureaucratic systems of accountability … have failed to produce rocketing standards.'

Illingworth located the origins of his health problems in the late 1980s devolution of responsibility to schools and the accompanying new inspection practices in the early 1990s. In his first headship,

> I was responsible for everything to do with teaching and learning and pupil welfare and I had a huge budget of three-and-a-half thousand pounds to spend on books and equipment in the school each year. The most significant accountability measure in those days was your link with your local education authority. Each school would have a local inspector and advisor who did have a job which was related to monitoring but it was also about supporting the school and looking at areas where the school needed to move on and develop.

In contrast, Illingworth said, in his next headship he had gradually accumulated new responsibilities – a budget of nearly a million pounds with total responsibility for all employment matters, management of new choice policies, the introduction of the National Curriculum and national testing, a different and more distanced form of inspection, and a period of budget contraction. He graphically described the kind of workload that resulted in his eventual breakdown.

> More and more, there has to be very precise evidence and justification for everything that's happening in a school and the introduction, this year, of the new OfSTED model where every year a head teacher is supposed to undertake this huge self-evaluation of the school. I was finding that in order to do that I either had to withdraw from important day-to-day running of the school or I had to do all that other work outside of

normal school day. So I was going in Saturdays; I was going in Sundays. I was spending my whole school holidays writing school stuff for evaluations; collecting evidence to support it all and at the same time the government decided that they wanted every school in the land to restructure their management responsibilities last year. Whether it was necessary or not, we all had to do it. At the same time, the government rightly insisted that all teachers needed some time outside the classroom for planning and preparation and assessment. A wonderful initiative but they didn't fund it, so we were then looking at how we could work and cut other budgets to provide that. All these things happening at the same time whilst I was trying to run a very, very busy school. So I was just sleeping – if I could get to sleep – or I was working. There was no time in my life when I wasn't either physically at work or mentally at work.

Illingworth went on to connect his own disillusionment and ill health with teacher and headteacher shortages. Predicting an impending crisis, Illingworth concluded his interview by suggesting the government needed to end the 'reign of terror … listen to teachers' and follow their lead. He revealed that he had attempted to dissuade his own children from entering the profession, and that the one that hadn't taken his advice was becoming disillusioned after only three years.

Illingworth deliberately offered himself to the media as an example of what he and the teacher and headteacher unions see as the contemporary cost of headship – stress, ill health and premature exit from post. He blamed the new system of quality management, the very thing that the fiction of Ian George shows as successful, as the reason – not for his or his school's failure – but for his departure from headship and the profession.

Sandra's story: leaving for something better

Sandra is head of a former mining village primary school. This is her third headship. Like Dave, her school is on a 'notice to improve' because the children's test results are not on target. Like Dave, she is angry about expectations that she sees as unrealistic and about prescriptive solutions that she is sure will not do what is being asked.

> I'm not decrying the government for their high expectations and standards. But we have the wrong people making decisions about how children learn and how children learn is really basic to everything that schools should be doing. We're still being funnelled down these very narrow strategies that just will not serve the needs of children who need more. Those capable students who are stamped level five when they come out of the womb it really won't matter what happens because they will get there.

The children from maybe 70 per cent of our families, who live in absolute disarray and have so many home and social indicators working against them – what are we genuinely doing for them other than probably making them feel worse about themselves because they don't hit these magic numbers? Our current Year 5 cohort has 35 children: 11 of them are 'School Action Plus' and ten have severe behaviour problems and another ten are for other educational additional needs so how am I going to hit 65 per cent with that cohort?

She and the school are under regular scrutiny about the processes that they are using to try to meet the targets that have been set for them.

I've got people meeting with me every six weeks – an external consultant and our own school improvement advisor and all this is being fed back to a primary strategy manager which is then being fed back to the DCFS to look at our progress towards 65 per cent this summer and if we don't hit that then what we've been threatened with is removal of the leadership, closure of the school and hard federation/soft federation; amalgamation. The works! The DCFS identified the school and the local authority sent us a copy of the letter. It is very draconian and really stark in its message. I have to say to a team who are breaking their necks that actually, because we are unlikely to get 65 per cent, I can't plan for the future of this school at the moment because I really don't know what it's going to be. I actually believe that the DCFS will insist that the local authority takes action. As recently as last week I sat in here with our link inspector and he said: 'You've just got to hit that 65 per cent in one subject.' I won't compromise the school's integrity or mine or my staff in any way and we will just do what we can do and what I keep saying is that we'll get as close to it as we can. But he keeps saying: 'But I'm sure you could.' And this just goes on and on and on and we had two years of ISP (Improving Schools Programme) before this as well. So we have to present at these meetings every six weeks about one cohort of 35 children and all the actions and everything that is happening down to groups of one and two; the booster groups we are running for them; the way we are organizing the teaching; how the support is being used.

Sandra is adamant that in this process there is more stick than carrot:

And do you know how much they've given for this? In 18 months they've given us £25,000 and they think that we should be incredibly grateful for that. £25,000 is just a drop in the ocean for a school like ours. Give us a proper injection – give us £250,000 and, my goodness, we'll make a difference.

She is also highly frustrated that, because of the time spent on trying to meet the targets and documenting what is happening, the very things that could be done to improve learning are not able to be done:

> They can go to hell with their personalized learning because they don't mean what they say. For me, personalized learning is about having a curriculum that is based upon the needs of our children and that's what we are going to do when we move forward. It's not about shoving pairs and small groups in two and three interventions through these programmes that are really narrow and actually do very little to build their confidence. As a school, what we're really trying to do at the moment is to look at a completely alternative way of coming at learning and I would have loved to do this three years ago but the staff weren't ready – but they are now. And we are looking at our whole curriculum restructure: how we look at academic guidance and that it will all come through thinking skills. The staff have to be brave enough to deliver that in the classroom: it's no good me saying this is how it's got to be. It's taken me two years to convince people that there is a better way of doing this. But that should be coming from somewhere else; that shouldn't be happening in isolated pockets and people shouldn't feel brave about doing it. It should be a right of young people that if we give them the skills they need which they can transfer to absolutely anything, then that will strengthen the learning processes for them because they will have this cross-application of everything that they do and they will feel more confidence.

Sandra is convinced that the progress that has been made in the school is related to the creative approaches that she has managed to initiate. She is frustrated that these are not recognized and that she is forced to do things that she knows are counter-productive:

> We have managed to get progress up over the last four years. I think that when I came our Curriculum Value Added was something like 96.4 and this year it was 99.2. So we can demonstrate that our children are making progress – but we're still doing all the measures by the wrong thing because what these kids need when they go from us is that they need to be constant learners, self-assured and absolutely sure that they can make the right contribution to anything and know where they are going. The current assessment process does nothing for them. We'll see groups of children; booster groups and I'm teaching every morning at the moment to try and hit these magic numbers and I am putting children through garbage. It isn't about giving up on their aspirations; I just know that it is the wrong way of doing it. I am not a negative person, believe it or not, but what I want to be able to do is to have the

freedom to do what I genuinely know these children want. I could get some of it wrong and I will and I have, but the lower you are down the league tables, the more prescriptive and narrow the curriculum becomes and the more that squeezes children out. It frightens them and turns them off and we are trying to balance that all the time. We are trying to give them their confidence and their self-respect; make sure relationships are good. And all the time we are working towards these very narrow targets. These children could do anything given the right amount of time and the right way of coming at them. So the system is just upside down.

Sandra has found that the improvement régime has compelled her to 'lead and manage' in a particular kind of way:

I'm protecting the staff and I'm only giving them the information that I think they can handle. I'm keeping some of the nasty stuff away from most of them. I've got a small group of four and we share absolutely everything because it's the only way I'd survive.

However, she is convinced that she cannot keep working this way:

It's the most revolting process I've ever been through. I'd never, ever want to find myself in a position like this again because I've actually had a very deep belief in the value of education throughout my entire life and I'm now doing things that I can't live with. This sort of turmoil is stifling in terms of my creativity and the way that I want to work with young people. And that is why I couldn't say, at the moment, that I would want to go into another headship. I am sick to the back teeth of working a system that is not fit for young people.

Sandra left the school shortly after talking to me. She is working in an advisory capacity where she can focus on the kind of leadership learning strategies she was unable to implement in what is, in all likelihood, her last school.

Unlike Ian George, Sandra did not have the freedom to innovate or the support to take creative risks: unlike him, she decided not to die, albeit emotionally and morally, in the job. She is now one of the growing number of heads for whom the job is unsustainable and un-doable.

The risks of accountability

When, in a song entitled 'The headmaster ritual', the melancholic Morrissey dubbed Manchester heads 'belligerent ghouls', accusing them of being 'spineless swines' with 'cemented minds', he reproduced a popular stereotype of headteachers as brutish child-haters. In the children's book *Matilda*, Roald Dahl (1989) created an equivalent in the vindictive Miss Trunchbull, who marched like a stormtrooper, radiated a dangerous heat like red-hot metal and was prone to whirling small girls around by their pigtails. Perhaps the ongoing subterranean presence of this sadistic image accounts for the fact that it is now not only possible but also very popular in some quarters to deal brutally with headteachers if they are seen to fall short of expectations.

The risks for headteachers that are produced through the new forms of accountability are created by policies intended to remove the risks of under-achievement for disadvantaged children. The cruel irony of achieving equity at the cost of some of the people who are most committed to achieving this outcome seems lost on policy-makers. Their eyes are fixed firmly on the kinds of measures that *appear* to show that a difference is being made. Time will tell whether these are indeed the measures which actually do make a difference for vulnerable children – and whether they were worth the costs of haemorrhaging headteachers from the schools in the most needy neighbour-hoods. It seems to be lost on policy-makers that these are the very schools where it is hardest to recruit headteachers and that the new 'sudden death' accountabilities are a major disincentive. One could hardly blame teachers for thinking that the risk of a successful application are simply too great.

III

More measures to address the supply problem

The book has argued that the supply and retention problems of headteachers are caused by a complex set of factors. It has suggested that succession planning is necessary but insufficient to tackle the reasons why teachers are reluctant to take on the job of headteacher in particular schools. It has led to the conclusion that the actual everyday work that headteachers must do *also* requires policy attention if teachers are to be convinced to apply and serving headteachers to stay.

The last chapter canvasses some policy options which address the realities of headteachers' daily work.

Chapter 8

Not now – we've got a head ache
Everyday policy for everyday work

Surveys of headteachers suggest that they enjoy high levels of job satisfaction, although this declines the longer they have been in post. Such reports are simultaneous with reports of overwork and high levels of stress.

We must assume that both satisfaction and stress can exist at the same time (see Chapter 4). Diana Pounder and Richard Merrill argue that this apparent paradox is because the emotional and philosophical commitment to the role and the rewards that these bring are always weighed up against experiences of, and judgements about, its 'do-ability' (Pounder and Merrill, 2001). Richard Sennett (1998, p. 82) suggests that 'people are more concerned about losses than gains when they take risks in their careers'. Moreover, the assessment of risks is less a process of rational calculation of the odds: it is 'something other than a sunny reckoning of the possibilities'. According to Sennett: 'The psychology of risk taking focuses quite reasonably on what might be lost.'

This perspective suggests that there is little point simply 'talking up' the position of headteacher in order to get more people to apply and/or to stay in post, while 'talking down' the job may well act as a powerful disincentive to potential applicants. It reinforces the notion that attention must be paid to the actual material conditions of headteacher's work. The job must not only *be* less arduous, time-consuming and risky, but also *be seen* to be so. Reducing the negative operational aspects of the headteacher role and work will not only sustain those in post, but also reassure those who are thinking about promotion that the risk of application is one worth taking. Policy-makers are not unaware of this, and across the world, a range of strategies to address the practices of school leadership/management are beginning to be put in place.

This chapter canvasses some of the different kinds of solutions that are on offer to make the work of headship more achievable. It reviews and summarizes arguments made in previous chapters and connects to possible 'supply problem' solutions.

The strategies offered to address headteachers' everyday work can be divided into two: (1) those that focus on the personal competencies used by individual heads to cope; and (2) those measures taken by others to alleviate or moderate the causes of their overwork and stress.

Taking charge of work – an individual approach

Recent reports suggest high levels of stress among headteachers (see Box 8.1). While teachers report that their stress is often related to children, head-teachers attribute it to external sources (McCormick, 1996).

Only a foolhardy few would argue that headteachers themselves are entirely to blame for the stress they experience, that they wilfully overwork and lack the skills to manage themselves. Some *do* suggest that heads find it difficult to 'turn off' their driving sense of obligation and duty (see Box 8.2).

Head-teachers *do* have to develop individual coping strategies in order to deal with workload, maintaining health, and ensuring that they have time for family, friends and leisure. Assisting heads to cope has been a strong focus for the NCSL in England, for a variety of UK professional media and for some involved in the provision of professional development for school leaders. Much of this kind of activity comes under the rubric of work–life balance, a term which is not universally accepted – some heads argue that work is an important part of their lives, and that the balance is between work, family and leisure.

A recent conference at the National College for School Leadership nominated a series of 'top tips' for achieving a better 'balance' (see Table 8.1).

Box 8.1 Headteachers and stress

A recent report by the NAHT staff absence insurers revealed that 38 per cent of all absence is through work-related stress amongst headteachers.[1] Head-teachers are a particularly vulnerable group and find themselves facing pressure from all sides – external pressure from the local authority, the community and school governors; and internal pressure from pupils and the school workforce. At the same time, headteachers have a responsibility to lead by example. In creating a healthy environment for pupils and staff alike, headteachers need to take the lead and practise what they preach.

(Teacher Support Network, 2006, p. 14)

Box 8.2 Doing it to themselves

Headteachers are not known as the world's best delegators. When the National College for School Leadership called for an end to the 'hero head' model this year, several of the attending headteachers missed it because they were too busy on their mobile phones, dealing with crises back at their schools.

(*Times Educational Supplement*, 21 September 2007, p. 18)

Table 8.1 Top tips from English heads

Personal strategies	*Professional strategies*
→ Getting a cleaner	→ Not going to every school event
→ Using a laundry service	→ Holding school meetings at 5.30
→ Using online shopping services	not at 7 pm
→ Handing all control of appointments	→ Only sending one set of data 'in' once
over to a secretary	and directing all other requests to that
→ Programming time at the gym	return
→ Instructing the secretary not to remove	→ Not filling out anything that isn't
the gym times even if instructed	mandatory
→ Booking all holidays overseas and well	→ Prioritizing actions and being prepared
in advance, ensuring there are hefty	to jettison things at the bottom of the list
penalties for cancellation	→ Not reading everything that arrives
→ Pausing between tasks to reflect	→ Not doing executive summaries for
(mini-meditations)	governors' meetings
→ Making time for professional reading	→ Reducing the number of committee
→ Turning off the computer	meetings in school

Source: Researcher notes

These were in addition to frequent, sometimes humorous, sometimes rueful, references to the necessity of a glass of wine at the end of the day to help unwind.

There is no doubt that headteachers' families also have to develop their own strategies for helping and for coping with absences. Support from home has been found to be a significant factor in stress management, and one study reports that 'on balance, home life's positive impact on work (in terms of inoculating people against the stresses and strains of the job) was greater than work's negative impact on home life' (Briner *et al.*, 2008, p. 68). This may of course be at some cost to the family members and to overall family functioning (see Box 8.3).

Some suggest that heads must become knowledgeable about their own and others' emotions. Belinda Harris (2007), for example, argues that school leaders must become much more emotionally aware of their own and others' vulnerabilities and must develop habits of self-care and ways of keeping themselves safe. They can benefit, she suggests, from forms of training that provide space, a language and experiences through which to come to deeper understandings of their own behaviours, values and attitudes. Being more emotionally aware also benefits the organization, she suggests, as leaders are better able to recognize, understand and deal with relationships, organizational dynamics and the inevitable crises and problems.

In addition to the headteacher and wider school leadership becoming more adept at managing the hours and nature of their work, there are also measures which others can take on their behalf.

Box 8.3 Family support

'I start every term with good intentions … my family does get resentful. They say you can find time for school, but not for us. You can get uptight in the job. So when I get home, all those emotions come to the surface. [My wife] calls me a grumpy old man. My daughters comment that I'm short-tempered.' Now, when he returns home they steer him into the conservatory to unwind on his own over a cup of coffee. 'When I look at other jobs in bigger schools [my wife] tells me money isn't everything,' he said. 'It's about quality of life as well.'

(*Times Educational Supplement*, 12 May 2006, p. 3)

Systemic and systematic policy approaches to headteachers' work

A study conducted for the UK Health and Safety Executive (Jordon *et al.*, 2003) concluded that organizations that are serious about the well-being of their workforce need to have top management commitment to a comprehensive stress prevention programme. This is developed through a participative approach to risk analysis, and the development of an action plan (stress prevention strategy): these frame the development and implementation of interventions at individual team and whole organization level. A modification of this approach, and one which fits with New Public Management, is the development of standards which local and regional organizations must meet and against which they can be measured (see Box 8.4).

There are serious questions about whether these kinds of health and safety standards are being met for the teaching profession as a whole. It is important to note that headteachers themselves are responsible for ensuring that these standards are met at school levels, and that the management practices of heads are often listed as a major stressor for teachers (Blase and Blase, 2004). This does not negate the fact that headteachers too suffer from stress and that *their* line managers must take responsibility for their health and safety.

Briner and colleagues (Briner *et al.*, 2008, p. 18) used the UK standards framework (in Box 8.4) to frame a survey of research and they report 'a fairly consistent association between low job control/autonomy and burnout … role conflict and role ambiguity have been found fairly consistently to be associated with burnout' and 'workload, general psychological demands and control have all been found to be associated with burnout and, in particular, emotional exhaustion'. These have all been reported by significant numbers of heads, as Chapters 3–7 have documented.

Briner *et al.* also conducted primary research into occupational stress, including a self-reporting diary study which focused on, *inter alia*, 10 headteachers (see Box 8.5).

Box 8.4 UK Health and Safety Executive Standards

Health and Safety Standards

1 *Demands* – Includes issues like workload, work patterns, and the work environment. The standard is that:

- Employees indicate that they are able to cope with the demands of their jobs; and
- Systems are in place locally to respond to any individual concerns.

2 *Control* – How much say the person has in the way they do their work. The standard is that:

- Employees indicate that they are able to have a say about the way they do their work; and
- Systems are in place locally to respond to any individual concerns.

3 *Support* – Includes the encouragement, sponsorship and resources provided by the organisation, line management and colleagues. The standard is that:

- Employees indicate that they receive adequate information and support from their colleagues and superiors; and
- Systems are in place locally to respond to any individual concerns.

4 *Relationships* – Includes promoting positive working to avoid conflict and dealing with unacceptable behaviour. The standard is that:

- Employees indicate that they are not subjected to unacceptable behaviours, e.g. bullying at work; and
- Systems are in place locally to respond to any individual concerns.

5 *Role* – Whether people understand their role within the organisation and whether the organisation ensures that the person does not have conflicting roles. The standard is that:

- Employees indicate that they understand their role and responsibilities; and
- Systems are in place locally to respond to any individual concerns.

6 *Change* – How organisational change (large or small) is managed and communicated in the organisation. The standard is that:

- Employees indicate that the organisation engages them frequently when undergoing an organisational change; and
- Systems are in place locally to respond to any individual concerns.

(Teacher Support Network, 2006, p. 23)

Box 8.5 A conflict between caring and management

[T]he head teachers in this sample conjured up the modern stereotype of teaching as a profession that is increasingly stifled by red-tape. They made frequent reference to needing to author a diverse range of reports and plans, in accordance with official requirement and deadlines. For the majority, this metaphorical mountain of paperwork came across as an unrewarding, burdensome and frequently overwhelming feature of the job. For example, one head teacher wrote of *'throwing away'* her briefcase *'years ago'* and substituting it with *'a supermarket crate'*, in order to accommodate all the paperwork which she needed to take home. Another wrote of how a particular report was *'hanging over'* her like the *'Sword of Damocles'*. A third noted a *'fear'* of the paperwork she was going to need to complete in response to meetings that day. And a fourth head teacher wrote of his annoyance at waking up early on a Sunday morning in order to work on the School Development Plan, and his worry about needing to *'get* [the] *plan done soon'*. In an otherwise fairly uneventful diary set, this diarist also circled 'burned out' and 'emotionally drained' in the emotion checklist on a day in which the two negative events consisted of, *'A teacher who was impatient with a parent'* and *'Amount of post and e-mails from local authority'*.

… paperwork also seemed to be seen as disproportionately time-consuming and stress-inducing compared to other, more important aspects of the head teacher's role. One diarist made the following comparison:

> Spoke to child today who said he hated himself and that he wanted to commit suicide – he is only eight. Seriously worried and have spoken to parent and teacher. Arranged to meet them tomorrow. This is the important stuff – not the piles of paper on my desk. But the paper and files make me feel more and more stressed as I hate not being in control of my work space.

In this quote, the child's crisis was experienced as emotionally demanding, but this was acceptable and perhaps even rewarding to deal with because it was important and meaningful in the context of her key responsibility (i.e. safeguarding the well-being of the children in her care). By contrast, the *'piles of paper'* were not emotionally demanding, but their very lack of importance and meaning seemed to render them arguably more stressful than the more emotionally taxing event which they were contrasted with. Paperwork therefore came across as a background stressor which was not emotionally demanding but which did have emotional consequences, not least because of its questionable value.

(Briner *et al.*, 2008, p. 63)

These results clearly indicate the kinds of role conflict that is the everyday experience of English heads, and in particular, the tension between caring and managerialism that is produced by contemporary policies and organizational arrangements. This finding is consistent with a significant number of studies (e.g. Blackmore, 2004; Maguire *et al.*, 2006; Reay and Ball, 2000; Saulwick Muller Social Research, 2004; Troman and Woods, 2000).

Getting a grip on headteacher overwork and stress

I now focus on some of the strategies that need to be included in interventions made on behalf of headteachers.

School systems that do attend to the health and well-being of teachers, and headteachers, must include: (1) monitoring and audit procedures; (2) holistic approaches to policy development; (3) support mechanisms; (4) appropriate and timely help; and (5) the development of preventive measures. This next section addresses each in turn.

Monitoring procedures

Most school systems have some data at their disposal which give them information about the health and well-being of their workforce – days taken off sick, reasons for long-term illness, claims for compensation on the grounds of work-related illness, and in some instances, regular surveys of workload. The annual teachers' work diary surveys undertaken by the School Review Board in England (Angle *et al.*, 2007; Office of Manpower Economics, 2000) is a good example of systemic and systematic monitoring of the hours and nature of work. The data give policy-makers in England *some* handle on the ways in which policies might be exacerbating or alleviating workload for different categories of employee and does pinpoint some potential trouble spots. But such data are not available in all educational jurisdictions; in many places this kind of work has to be especially commissioned (e.g. in Canada, Blouin, 2005; and Australia, Saulwick Muller Social Research, 2004), rather than being an inbuilt aspect of public management human relations systems.

However, no educational systems appear to have yet moved to the stage where they *regularly* monitor well-being, or ill-health which has not yet reached crisis levels.[2] Stress downgrades the body's immune system and increases vulnerability to a range of pathogens. It can play out in a range of symptoms which range from chronic headaches and indigestion to chronic hypertension, depression, and cardiac disease. Minor illnesses and stress may *never* reach the stage of claims for compensation, but can seriously detract from the quality of life of the sufferer, as well as their actual job performance.

Studies of headteacher stress, health and well-being appear to always be one-off commissioned audits. The National College for School Leadership in England for example has had an ongoing commitment to addressing the 'work/life balance' of headteachers: it commissioned just such a study in 2007.[3] The study suggested that, in comparison to other occupations, headteachers suffered high levels of stress. In saying this, it is important to remember that, in absolute terms, headteachers are part of a relatively wealthy and healthy middle class: epidemiological studies (e.g. Wilkinson, 2005) show that the more unequal the society, the greater the health problems associated with being poor. However, teachers, nurses and managers *do* report the highest levels of occupational stress (Smith *et al.*, 2000).

An education system which takes seriously the well-being of headteachers will have in place a system to regularly audit details of working hours, stress levels, well-being, and any local initiatives to address them. This kind of information is an organizational bottom line: it is critical for understanding the overall epidemiological impact of organizational practices and policy changes.

Holistic approaches to policy development

When education systems develop policies, they generally bring together a set of information and a series of 'positions' from various 'interests'. Through the processes of policy development and negotiation, policy-makers develop specifications for the realization of policy goals. Most policies therefore do have specific budget allocations for training and development and/or for new equipment and plant and/or for specialist staff and/or support of a particular kind. Such costs are generally calculated in terms of the impact on central budget, although in some cases, costs at school level might also be part of the computation.

But many policies carry costs which are relatively hidden from the gaze of central policy-makers. Three examples from England will suffice to illustrate this:

1 When primary planning time (a time for teachers when someone else took their class) was introduced into primary schools in England, additional funds were provided for staffing (although there is debate about whether it was adequate).[4] However, additional administrative costs – of recruiting, appointing and managing additional staff, as well as timetabling and supervising them – were omitted from the budgetary considerations.

2 The introduction of the school self-evaluation discussed in Chapter 7 required the development of new centralized data systems and continuous audit of school data. These costs were offset by money saved on actual inspections. However, what was omitted from the calculations was the considerable additional school administrative time, generally the head and other members of the senior management team, taken at school level in order to develop and maintain the mandated online data.

3 When it was agreed to take tasks away from teachers to relieve their workload, schools were allocated additional funds to employ teaching assistants.

Schools were generally pleased to have this flexibility and many initiated interesting 'staff mix' practices as a result (Gunter *et al.*, 2007). However, not all of the tasks removed from teachers were directed towards teaching assistants and some ended up in the school front office as additional workload (Thomson *et al.*, 2007). Office time either had to be increased, or heads had to decide to reduce services in other areas.

These are the 'hidden costs' of devolved management, audit and policy implementation (see Chapters 4 and 7).

Central policies often have 'knock-on' effects which must simply be absorbed into the leadership and management of the school. Much of what headteachers describe as their additional workload, and the unending array of paperwork, derives from just such dispersal of formerly centralized tasks.

One systemic approach to this problem is to introduce a Workload Impact Statement as part of all policy development. This would require the public and transparent computation of all policy costs at central, regional and local levels prior to any finalization of the policy. It would provide a mechanism for education systems to examine the number and frequency of policy changes and how they interact. The workload and work of headteachers and senior leaders and managers would thus become a visible aspect of the policy development process.

Support mechanisms

There are a number of measures which educational systems can take to support headteachers in their work. They can, for example, provide a range of coping courses which address the personal/organizational interface – time and stress management, coping with crises, how to handle the media, dealing with difficult staff and parents. They can provide administrative support for headteachers' self-initiated networks. Some school governing bodies supplement these policies with specific undertakings about the well-being of headteachers (e.g. Partnership Project, undated).

One mechanism which gets the vote of many headteachers is the provision of a 'critical friend', also called a coach or mentor in different jurisdictions. The critical friend is generally someone who also has had experience as a headteacher and who has no particular agenda other than to provide a listening ear and counsel. Headteachers value this relationship precisely because of the loneliness of the position. Even if the senior leadership/management team works closely and collaboratively, many heads still feel isolated – it is they who have to shoulder responsibility for the school, as the person in the 'top job' they carry the expectations, hopes and fears of staff, the school community and the system. They must appear to be strong and positive even when they do not feel it. Tim Brighouse once noted to an NCSL conference for aspiring heads:[5]

[I]t's the responsibility of existing heads never to acknowledge when somebody says 'You've got an impossible job', which they do in the middle of a crisis. It's very tempting to think 'Well, hell, I have got an impossible job' and say nothing or nod or kind of let people think that it is an impossible job because it isn't, and they know it's not. It's challenging, of course it's challenging. But the moment they acknowledge it's an impossible job is the moment they are saying to that person and everybody else who listens to it 'I'm not sure I really want that job'. It's a tremendously tempting thing to do and I think we should avoid it at all costs.

Many heads find that the requirement to keep silent and strong is psychologically exhausting and professionally frustrating. The provision of a critical friend breaks the inbuilt isolation of their position and provides a helpful sounding board. Unlike networks with colleague headteachers, which are also of value and valued by many heads, there is no sense of competition with a critical friend, and no risk that anything that is said will be repeated to anyone else (see Box 8.6).

Another way to avoid headteacher burnout is via adequate leave provisions. Australian headteachers are fortunate to work in a country where there is a universal national system of 'long service leave' for all employees. Ten days leave is accrued for every year of service, and employees are able to access this leave after ten years when they have twenty working weeks available to them. The budgetary tradeoff for this provision lies in the specific nature of the Australian welfare state. All those who work are expected

---

Box 8.6 How Dave has coped

The local authority gave me some money so I had a consultant who is an ex inner city head and now she supports schools in urban contexts. So, for a start, she's got some relevant experience but I was saying to her that I need to know if I'm crap; I need to know if I can't do this ... she doesn't come in and say: you should do this or that. We talk about things and we will talk every couple of weeks when she comes in for an hour or so. It's just an opportunity to get another view really. And there was a lot of reflection on the school and trying to balance the need to meet all these targets with looking at the students and what it means to be a student and we are now very focused with the kids and the parents on what it means to be a student.

... the local authority now doesn't think paying for a coach is a good thing to do and I'm very disappointed with that. I'm now paying for her for next term.

(Dave, secondary head, UK, see Chapter 7)

to contribute to the costs of what in some other nations is provided free for everyone: all health and welfare services are means-tested but a compensatory range of benefits have been built up around employment (Castles, 1991). The provision of long service leave provides a period of time in which those who work can 'recharge' and reinvigorate themselves. The thinking behind long service leave equates it roughly to the regular retreats that priests undergo in order to attend to their own spiritual and physical well-being. For those in the professions where they must give of themselves, long service leave provides precisely that kind of replenishment.

Some Canadian teachers, while not in a situation where they have long service leave, have been able to bargain for a scheme where they extend a four-year salary over five years, taking the fifth year as leave. The employer has the full fifth year of salary to use in order to pay for the one-year replacement. In education, these one-year positions often serve as the means for teachers to get experience in a promotion position prior to obtaining a permanent step up.

Combinations of support provisions could be bundled up with salary as headteacher well-being packages – gym membership, the provision of a coach, access to well-being training and development and some arrangements for sabbatical leave for example. Well-being packages would signal to applicants that the employer/governing body is prepared to take some responsibility for their health and safety and to assist them to look after themselves. This could well prove as attractive to some potential applicants as a very big salary or performance bonuses.

Appropriate and timely assistance

Sometimes heads, like teachers, do get to the point where they need more than a fortnightly conversation with a coach, and it is critical that educational systems provide professional counselling systems which are easily accessible and confidential. Such counselling services also need to combine elements of professional advice, and so it is important that when heads access such services that they find themselves working with someone who understands the professional requirements of their position. Clinical qualifications are necessary but also specific positional knowledges.

If heads are at the point where they are facing serious physical or mental health issues, then it is critical that they do not stay at work through guilt or because there is no-one else to do the work. But if headteachers leave suddenly there is a domino effect as those who 'act up' may well find themselves equally stressed and overworked within a short space of time (Cosgrove, 2000). It is vital that employers/governing bodies have plans in place to 'understudy' all positions, including the headteacher. This may not simply be a matter of giving the most senior member of the leadership team the responsibility for 'acting up', but could be a way of ensuring that all members of the team take turns to look after the school for short and longer periods of time. More innovative approaches are also possible (see Box 8.7). This is the only way to ensure that in emergencies there are clear roles and responsibilities, and the school is not thrown into disarray if the head has to suddenly take time off.

But support must go further than an individualized approach. It is vital that there is more discussion between heads and their local/central line managers about what it is they need. Systems that are serious about supporting heads to manage everyday work need to have better ways of finding out what is required. They must monitor their own levels of support and provision. Here are two propositions which illustrate the kinds of conversations that need to occur between heads and local authorities/districts/regions:

1   There may not be a lot that can be done to prevent the kinds of everyday and unanticipated crises I discussed in Chapters 5 and 6, but it is clear from the stories of the heads that more might be done in the longer term to assist heads to work through the effects of such events. A specific 'troubleshooting' or 'ombudsperson' officer could be allocated to schools who experience the effects of natural and unnatural disasters. This officer, independent of architectural and building services, could support heads to manage through any periods of inaction, and intervene where heads are struggling to make headway against bureaucratic lassitude.
2   It may be unlikely that one major source of headteacher heartburn – the actions of the media – will change. Until the media return to a set of

---

Box 8.7 Preventing a leadership crisis

I took two terms long service leave out a couple of years ago and we didn't replace the principal. It was about 4 years into the school, right, and we had a relatively stable group of heads of campus and part of the thinking was that, if you replace the principal you would expect it to go to one of the senior people. But if you do that you could well set up the perception of a hierarchy and that would then mean that when I'm not there that it would defer to that person as a de facto deputy. I didn't want that to happen. So, what we did is, we put everyone up a rung, and then we spent all the rest of the money on special ed. We also identified a group of specific tasks and divided it up that way.

PT: And when there was a crisis? They all met together and decided?
Head: Sorted it out, yeah.
PT: So you really don't need to be there at all (laughs)
Head: Well, very often I'm not!

(Head multi-campus all ages school, Australia)

ethics which encompass the consequences of their reportage, then heads will still have to engage with local and national media who are more directed towards circulation than a more generous notion of the public good, and the public 'right to know'. However, courses for headteachers in dealing with the media might be available as a training entitlement, together with project management and crisis management, to be taken up at a time when it is convenient. Headteachers might also have, as part of the systemic services available to them, immediate access to professional media advice if they find themselves in a crisis situation.

Current policy approaches emphasize the need for schools to regularly consult with and survey their school communities, but this practice needs to extend upwards. **Education systems need to more regularly audit the levels of support and service they provide to schools. Regular 'satisfaction surveys' or '360-degree audits' of systemic service would allow heads to discuss the specific support requirements they have of local and central authorities.**

The development of alternative models of work

There are emergent models of headteacher's work that are different from the lone and lonely hero head.

One popular strategy for reducing headteacher workload is 'distributed leadership' (Spillane, 2006), a system through which teachers in both formal and informal positions have the independence and authority to initiate change activities.

It is important to note that this is not a new idea. In the early 1980s, Patrick Whitaker (1983) wrote about the importance of the primary headteacher 'spreading the load' and noted the general reluctance of primary heads to 'involve their colleagues in policy making, staff supervision and the management of innovation' (ibid., p. 85). This he attributed to the persistence of paternalism in heads who saw the school as 'my school' and lacked confidence in the abilities of others. They thus closely supervised as many activities as possible and retained the last word on all matters. Whitaker argued for the principle of delegation which may indeed be the most common practical realization of 'distributed leadership'. The questions to be asked are, which tasks are to be distributed, to whom, and with what effects.

There is considerable debate about the notion of distributed leadership and its accuracy and adequacy as a concept (Gunter, 2005; Harris, 2003; Lambert, 1998). It is suggested that over time, teacher leadership has become more instrumental (Warren Little, 2003), and that while teacher teaming is good for most, some report an increase in their workloads, a loss of professional autonomy, and the emergence of damaging competition between teams for resources, recognition and power (Johnson, 2003). Some headteachers suggest that distributed leadership is simply a way of sharing out monitoring and audit activities through the creation of teams, and that in many contexts, the English case being the most extreme (see Chapter 7), heads are simply not able to give away responsibility, and nor are they prepared to give away their power. A democratic approach to school leadership/management, by contrast, focuses on the way in which decisions are made, by whom and on what, as well as who has the capacities to initiate discussions, debates, plans and activities (Begley and Zaretsky, 2004; Hatcher, 2005; Moller, 2006; Moos and Mac-beath, 2004). Delegation combined with democracy may be the most potent combination for easing pressure on heads but may prove to be a difficult combination to realize.

There are also various models of co-principalship and of executive head-ships where one head takes responsibility for another school or for a series of campuses. Depending on whether these sites retain their own governing bodies, budgets and staffing complements, these arrangements (called federations in England) can be more or less thorough (hard and soft federation being the English descriptors).

Marion Court (1998, 2003a, 2003b, 2004) has been examining existing models of headship and seeking some way of defining these differences. She suggests that there is a 'continuum of leadership' that she describes as:

- *Sole leadership*: In sole leadership, one person, as the real and titular head, has the dominant voice and leadership is not shared.
- *Supported leadership*: Supported leadership (characterized sometimes as the 'patron' approach, or consultative leadership) exists where the recognized single leader draws on and acknowledges input and advice from a wide range of people.
- *Dual leadership*: Dual leadership involves a partnership between two people, both recognized as the leaders.
- *Shared leadership*: Shared leadership is diffuse– a property shared to some degree by all persons and groups involved in the collaboration (Court, 2003b, p. 6). According to Court, this is leadership which is holistic and purposive, and its concerted action constitutes more than the sum of its parts.

While co-headship might enhance role commitment, reduce role conflict and thus produce greater job satisfaction (Eckman, 2006), federation and co-headships do not necessarily shift the *burden* of leadership a great deal. In the case of federations these may actually increase the level of work undertaken by the executive head, or, as in the case of the head in Box 8.7, reduce it considerably. This is because in forced arrangements, there can be new communication problems and deep concerns about loss of individual identity and power to deal with. Heads may also find themselves going to more meetings outside of their own school in the case of federations and clusters, or within school in the case of co-headships. Co-headships are not necessarily a panacea, and they need 'buy-in' from school staff, governors and the local authority/district (Grubb and Flessa, 2006).

However, more generous administrative and middle management infrastructures made possible through such arrangements can productively combine with more democratic decision-making structures and the generation of new educational cultures to reduce the wear and tear on heads (see Box 8.8).

But if the heads' workload is to be genuinely reduced, it relies on a more holistic approach to change which goes beyond the most senior level of the school (see Box 8.9). It also goes beyond simple delegation to fundamental changes in the ways in which most things get done – even learning. In redesigned schools, many staff have to acquire new autonomies, capacities and responsibilities.

Box 8.8 Everyday practices of co-headship

In our deputies' roles I was always very clearly delineated as curriculum and staff professional development and student professional development and he was always timetable and daily administration. So we just kept those delineations in our current role. We both pick up aspects of daily admin and we have always picked up pastoral care, and the whole thing of discipline. So we work very closely with parents, and whoever is there takes the call and begins the process. Keeps the other informed.

In the beginning, we thought we had to inform each other about everything in that first year and now we know we don't. The quick note, the quick message, and we work very much through our secretary.

Our secretary changed this year so she is finding out about the process and what it means to be working with two instead of one and I think it was probably more problematic for the previous secretary who had always worked for one to suddenly think 'I have to be repeating information. I have to be doing two copies of everything'. All of that had to be sorted out in the first few months. There were initial shufflings and siftings and sortings which were very normal. So we had a shared calendar on file which I never kept up to date because I had my desk diary. I had my diary in my bag. Those sorts of things which probably drove everybody mad so in the end, you know, just say 'Look, my desk diary is there, grab it when you've got a minute, update the calendar because we realize we don't have to do everything ourselves.'

So the role of the co-principals' secretary is really crucial to the success of the process. It really is. It can't be underestimated. Keeps things balanced. Keeps people reminded. Keeps things on track. And from that point on it started to work quite well.

(Co-head, secondary, Australia)

Box 8.9 A 'soft federation' in action

The schools are in a rural wheat and wool region that is declining in population and economic prosperity. There are five towns spread across some 200 km, each with their own high school or area school (an area school is a combined primary and secondary). Each of the schools struggled to provide the range of curriculum students expected of their public school. Face-to-face teaching, particularly in the senior years and for specialist subjects such as language other than English, was supplemented by the state distance education provision, which had advanced considerably since pedal wireless and correspondence lessons, but which nevertheless was seen by local families as a poor second best to what was routinely on offer to students in the city.

The school principals and local district Superintendent organized a series of meetings with governing bodies and local communities and won agreement that they should become a formal curriculum and staff sharing network – the Northern Regional Consortium. Their goal was to offer the range of learning experiences to country students equivalent to that available in the city. In practical terms, this meant:

- appointing curriculum middle managers to the cluster but based in one school with cluster 'faculty' meetings held once per term rotating around each site. Some middle managers also changed their base school site every second year.
- wiring each school so that there were audio visual and Internet connections between each site such that it was possible to teach across sites using distance methods;
- harmonizing timetables across sites by building the five timetables through cooperative negotiation;
- appointing subject specialist teachers to the cluster so that they could run extended classes of viable sizes. Distance technologies were supplemented with regular combined face-to-face whole classes and teachers were able to move sites often enough to ensure that each site had some face-to-face teaching during the year.
- establishing some joint administrative procedures to share timing of school renovations and all but emergency repairs, and joint purchase of equipment and supplies;
- establishing a shared budget for cluster activities, e.g. additional travel between sites using school buses, running shared governance meetings once per term, establishing cluster working parties and holding joint principals meeting once a month. Joint whole school staff development was also undertaken regularly. A cluster student advisory body was formed and through regular meetings, lobbied successfully for a greater range of cluster-based sporting and cultural activities.

The cluster soon offered a wider range of subject choice than any single site in the city.

Principals avoided having to make any staff redundant and turned around the views of a country community fast becoming very disillusioned with their public schools. From feeling that the job was one of managing an unpopular decline, the principals collectively redesigned the educational provision, and in so doing, aspects of their jobs.

This example is important in three ways:

- it disrupts the notion that principals' work is/ought to be confined to one site and suggests that in some circumstances, looking inside the school for solutions may not be what is required. It offers the idea that shared leadership may be horizontal (across schools) as well as vertical.
- the importance of establishing new systems to build new ways of doing things is very clear. Without changed arrangements for staffing, finances, time, buildings and governance, the cluster would have failed. Without building in various kinds of meetings, movements around schools and particular kinds of conversations, the cluster would have failed
- the significance of the goal was a key to bringing about change. This was not a 'vision' *per se*, or a mission. Rather, it was a profoundly pragmatic exercise around which there were huge emotional investments and a remarkable confluence of needs and interests.

The cluster provided a solution for the different problems of teachers, students and their families – and the state system which managed to more efficiently attract, induct and retain teachers in a country location, and demonstrate improved student achievement.

(Thomson and Blackmore, 2006, pp. 167–8)

Education systems which are serious about addressing the ways in which the nature and role of the head's job cause overwork and stress should support systematic and continuously evaluated trials of school redesign. Such redesigns need to encompass innovations in staff organization, curriculum and pedagogical arrangements and decision-making.

But is school redesign in itself enough? Some researchers (Smithers and Robinson, 2006, p. v) suggest that the current difficulty in recruiting head-teachers does *not* demand a massive change in the nature of headship. They argue, in the case of England, that 'the government should look to itself and ask whether its reforming zeal and policy of pressure from the centre' is the real issue.

In conclusion: tough on the supply problem, tough on the causes of the supply problem

This book has addressed the supply problem and its dimensions. It has suggested that succession planning is a necessary but insufficient response. Using the notion of risk, it has proposed that teachers assess the headteacher position as they see it, and make choices about whether the positives about the job are sufficient to counter balance its negative aspects.

This book suggests, together with others, that particular pressures arise from the ways in which everyday work, and the trio of devolution, testing, audit and inspection, and league tables come together in mediatised contexts. The English case (Chapter 7) is simply the most extreme example. There is mounting debate in England about testing and league tables, with independent schools and parliamentarians joining professional organizations and researchers to argue for change. However, shifting just one part of the organizational architecture will not suffice, and may actually, as in the case of the change from external inspection to school self-evaluation and light touch inspection, only make things worse for the schools struggling to improve.

The book argues, in concert with many others, that at least some of the cause of headteachers' early departure from post, and the reluctance of some teachers to apply for the position, derives from the nature of heads' everyday work. The head's daily régime of 'encounters' with all and sundry is necessary and time-consuming. Heads have no choice but to meet crises and unpredictable random events head on.

Policy-makers can make meeting these everyday requirements more or less possible. And policy-makers could simply choose not to keep pushing more and more tasks onto schools and generating policies at breakneck speed. Many schools and heads just cannot change that quickly. 'Not now, we'll wait till later' is the policy rhetoric heads hope to hear.

Policy-makers add unnecessary pressures to the headteachers' role. High expectations often translate into unrealistic requirements. Fictions of hero heads with charismatic leadership are taken to be universal possibilities.

School systems are of course aware that heads are under pressure. While providing personal, professional and school support for headteachers is necessary, it is not enough in and of itself. While school redesign can go some way towards alleviating the ways in which work is organized across schools, it too is not enough.

Policy-makers must look much more seriously at the question of retention of headteachers. Local and central policymakers *must* find ways of avoiding rapid turnover of headteachers since length of time in post is inextricably entwined with the sustained improvement of both individual schools and school systems (Hargreaves and Fink, 2006). Rather than letting heads quietly retire, or limp away from their posts (Lacey and Gronn, 2007), policy-makers need to know much more about who is leaving and why. They then need to establish ongoing systems for monitoring headteacher departure rates and reasons.

School systems do face some serous risks in relation to the supply problem. There is thus a need for serious 'joined up thinking' about where there are problems in attracting heads and why, what is being asked and expected of headteachers, the data about premature exit, early retirement, and ill-health, and the current policy régime. Failure to address this holistic ecology of schooling and the role that headteachers play in it, will at best only partially resolve the supply problem.

This book proposes that without some substantive changes in the everyday demands made of headteachers, those teachers who are weighing up the risks of application will continue to perceive problems and risks they may not be willing to take on.

Notes

Introduction: headship is a risky business

1 A black economy operates almost entirely outside of the orthodox official economy, while a shadow economy often supports it; the alleged systematic use of Eastern European builders on large building sites in Britain is an example of a shadow economy.

1 Getting a head: the problem of supply

1 See Chapman (2005) and 20 OECD country reports on http://www.oecd.org/document/53/0,3343,en_2649_39263231_38520905_1_1_1_1,00.html (accessed 30 June 2008). There is currently no reported shortage in the Asia Pacific (1997). However, some of the policy changes which are reported to be implicated in the shortages in English-speaking countries are now being introduced into these nation-states. It thus remains to be seen whether these initiatives might produce in these places a similar reluctance among teachers to apply for headship.
2 Where there are isolated families of children the Australian solution is not a school, but distance education.

2 A heads up: solutions to the supply problem

1 See http://www.aasa.org/publications/content.cfm?ItemNumber = 4551 for further details of assessment centres (accessed 16 April 2008). These are also in use in England and Australia.
2 The NSCL commissioned a survey from MORI which was reported in the *TES* on 6 June 2006 (p. 7), and then again at the 2008 annual conference, as saying that the majority of the public would be happy to see business leaders, police and military officers running schools.

3 Head of the pack: the problem of great expectations

1 Content analysis is a form of categorising and quantifying texts (see Silverman, 1993).
2 See www.redesigningheadship.org: the site has a range of resources on offer including spoof and more desirable forms of job advertisements.

4 Head work: the problem of time on tasks

1 There are studies which contradict this claim, for example, Robinson and Godbey (1997) who in the 1990s suggested Americans actually have more leisure than fifty years previous. Claims of overwork were 'fashionable' rather than reality.
2 Keith's story about money is not uncommon. Many heads are driven to distraction by historical budgetary problems or mistakes in budgetary allocations from the dispensing agency.
3 *The Age*, 18 August 2003. Reprinted on principals association website: www.acppa. catholic.edu.au/news/topics/14–3_barger.html. Accessed 13 November 2006.

5 Head land: the problem of the time-consuming and predictable

1 See also www.telegraph.co.uk/core/Content/. Accessed 21 April 2008
2 See www.gtce.org.uk/standards/hearing/disciplinaries/ I accessed the site on 21 April 2008 and categorized the offences listed on that date.
3 I know, I've been there three times – an alcoholic teacher I never ever pinned down, a teacher stealing from colleagues to pay for an addiction, and another who had an inappropriate relationship with a student. All created divisions among the staff, some of whom thought I was weak for not acting soon enough, and others who thought I was unfair because of the action I took.
4 These examples come from field notes of conversations with heads about Public Private Partnerships, Nova Scotia, August 2002.

6 Heads or tails: the problem of controlling the unpredictable

1 In February 2008, 100,000 people were still living in trailers which contained formaldehyde, a known carcinogen. See www.abcnews.go.com/print?id = 4293398. Accessed 24 March 2008.
2 See www.nytimes.com/2007/09/17/arts/design/17ther.html. Accessed 24 March 2008.
3 See the UK Cabinet website, *uk resilience* on www.ukresilience.info/response/recovery_guidance _case_studies/bl_yh_floods.aspx. Accessed 24 April 2008.
4 See www.24dash.com/news/Local_Government/2007-07-05-Flood-hit-Hull-is-UK-s-forgottencity. Accessed 24 April 2008.
5 See www.contractjournal.com/Articles/Article.aspx?liArticleID = 58226. Accessed 27 April 2008.
6 See Ganston case study on www.ukresilience.info/response/recovery_guidance_case_studies/ bl_yh_floods.aspx. Accessed 24 April 2008
7 West Bridgford School in Nottingham recently experienced just this, and the head was forced to cancel a proposed information session for parents amid fears it would be the subject of a large protest (*Evening Post* 23 March 2007, p. 1).
8 See wikipedia for a description. www.en.wikipedia.org/wiki/Snowtown_murders. This case is particularly important to me. I was the head of School 3 at the time the murders were committed and one of the murderers and two of the victims were former students. The school faced the house where the two bodies were found and we had experienced ongoing problems with its occupants who mysteriously disappeared in circumstances that are now clear.
9 See www.en.wikipedia.org/wiki/soham_murders
10 *Guardian*, 16 April 2008. Available on www.guardian.co.uk/world/2008/apr/16/5?gusrc = rss&feed = networkfront. Accessed 23 April 2008.
11 See *Education Guardian*, 15 April 2008. www.education.guardian.co.uk/higher/worldwide/ story/0,2273749,00.html. Accessed 15 April 2008.
12 ABC News, 23 May 2008. See www.abc.net.au/news/stories/2008/05/23/2253287.htm. Accessed 23 May 2008,

13 For example, a Google search (28 April 2008) of 'school stabbing 2008' had 246,000 hits; 'school fire' returned 12,700,000 and 'school shooting' returned 1,980,000. Assuming that most of these are multiple reports and discussions rather than events, there are still a lot of hits which are actual occurrences.

14 My own knowledge of what happened to my colleagues when President of a headteachers' association leads me to this view, as do numerous conversations with officers in district offices and local authorities. Any education system which does not conduct regular health checks with heads – and that is pretty well all of them – to ask what kinds of predictable and unpredictable crises and emergencies they have dealt with is not keeping an occupational health and safety eye on key employees. See Chapter 9.

15 See NCSL research associate report, *Critical Incidents: Effective Responses and the Factors Behind Them* (Mander, 2008).

7 Off with their heads: the extreme sport of new accountabilities

1 See BBC news on news.bbc.co.uk/go/pr/fr/-/1/hi/education/7442361.html Accessed 9 June 2008.

2 See www.telegraph.co.uk/core/Content/display/Printable.jhtml;jsessionid = K0H543I ... Accessed 16 July 2007.

3 I have written about Dave before (Thomson, 2008a, 2008b).

4 The interview was from a radio programme called *On the Ropes*. The quotations here are from a transcript of the interview recorded from the actual broadcast.

8 Not now – we've got a head ache

1 Cited in the text as Schools Advisory Service, 'October 2005 Absence Survey'.

2 There is no ideal 'off the shelf' well-being audit tool available for educational systems to use. The most common type of instrument used is a form of self reporting such as a questionnaire. These are generally designed for research, not organizational purposes. Critics of such approaches (e.g. Rick *et al.*, 2001) argue that the questions which respondents have to answer are often too narrow and the instruments lack rigour. They suggest that measuring stress in the workplace could be enhanced by the addition of measures such as observations, analysis of tasks and job descriptions. Moreover, organizations need to do the following:

> consider developing their own measures which should be:
>
> - focused on particular organisations and jobs or roles
> - more specific and shorter
> - based on local knowledge and understanding of the context
> - informed by best practice (e.g. frequency based response formats)
> - incorporated into some form of risk management framework.
>
> (Rick *et al.*, 2001, p. 82)

3 At the time of writing the study, conducted by Professor Cary Cooper, was unpublished. I saw some of the results presented at a NCSL conference; these slides are available on www.ncsl.org.uk/leading practice

4 PhD work in progress by Bob Curtis.

5 A transcript of the Brighouse talk was available on the *Tomorrow's Leaders Today* section of the NCSL website on 5 April 2008.

Bibliography

All journals and newspapers as shown in the text.

Ah Nee-Benham, M., and Cooper, J. (1998). *Let my spirit soar! Narratives of diverse women in school leadership*. Thousand Oaks, CA: Sage.

Ainscow, M., and West, M. (Eds). (2006). *Improving urban schools: Leadership and collaboration*. Buckingham: Open University Press.

Alberti, J. (Ed.). (2004). *Leaving Springfield: The Simpsons and the possibility of oppositional culture*. Detroit: Wayne State University Press.

Alder, J. (2007). Voices and values: New Labour's failing schools policies 1997–2005. Unpublished Ed D thesis. Keele University, Keele.

Ang, I. (1985). *Watching Dallas: Soap opera and the melodramatic imagination*. London: Methuen.

Angle, H., Gilbey, N., and Belcher, M. (2007). *Teachers' workload diary survey, March 2007*. London: Office of Manpower Economics, School Teachers Review Board.

Angus, L. (2004). Globalisation and educational change: Bringing about the reshaping and renorming of practice. *Journal of Education Policy, 19*(1), 23–41.

Apple, M. (2001). *Educating the "right" way: Markets, standards, God and inequality*. London: RoutledgeFalmer.

Australian Education Union (AEU). (2007). *State of our schools survey*. Melbourne: AEU.

Bacchi, C. L. (1999). *Women, policy and politics: The construction of policy problems*. London: Sage.

Baker, B. D., and Cooper, B. S. (2005). Do principals with stronger academic backgrounds hire better teachers? Policy implications for improving high-poverty schools. *Educational Administration Quarterly, 41*(3), 449–79.

Ball, S. (1998). Big policies/small world: An introduction to international perspectives in education policy. *Comparative Education, 34*(2), 119–30.

—— (2007). *Education plc: Understanding private sector participation in public sector education*. London: Routledge.

—— (2008). *The education debate*. Bristol: The Policy Press.

Banks, S. (2004). *Ethics, accountability and the social professions*. Hampshire: Palgrave.

Barker, D. (2003). *Lost quality in emergent leadership? The identification and development of inexperienced teachers as future school leaders*. Nottingham: NCSL.

Barty, K., Thomson, P., Blackmore, J., and Sachs, J. (2005). Unpacking the issues: Researching the shortage of school principals in two states of Australia. *Australian Educational Researcher, 32*(3), 1–14.

Baskwill, J. (2003). Is there room for the girls in the boys club? A study of women elementary school administrators in Nova Scotia, Canada. Unpublished PhD thesis. University of South Australia, Adelaide.

Bauman, Z. (1998). *Work, consumerism and the new poor*. Buckingham: Open University Press.

—— (2002). *Society under siege*. Cambridge: Polity.

Bauman, Z., and May, T. (2001). *Thinking sociologically* (2nd ed.). Malden, MA: Blackwell Publishing.

Beaudin, B. Q., Thompson, J. S., and Jacobson, L. (2002, 1–5 April). The administrator paradox: More certificated, fewer apply. Paper presented at the American Educational Research Association Annual Meeting, New Orleans.

Beck, U. (1992). *Risk society: Towards a new modernity*. London: Sage.

Beck, U., Giddens, A., and Lash, S. (1994). *Reflexive modernisation: Politics, tradition and aesthetics in the modern social order*. Stanford, CA: Stanford University Press.

Begley, P., and Zaretsky, L. (2004). Democratic school leadership in Canada's public school systems: Professional value and social ethic. *Journal of Educational Administration, 4*(6), 640–55.

Bilton, C. (2007). *Management and creativity: From creative industries to creative management*. Oxford: Blackwell.

Blacklock, K. (2002). Dealing with an incompetent teacher. *APPA Gold Matters, 3*(3), APPA online member materials. Reprinted from NEASP.

Blackmore, J. (1999). *Troubling women: Feminism, leadership and educational change*. Buckingham: Open University Press.

—— (2004). Restructuring educational leadership in changing contexts: A local/global account of restructuring in Australia. *Journal of Educational Change, 5*(267–88).

Blackmore, J., and Sachs, J. (2007). *Performing and reforming leaders: Gender, educational restructuring and organisational change*. New York: State University of New York Press.

Blackmore, J., Thomson, P., and Barty, K. (2006). Principal selection: Homosociability, the search for security and the production of normalised principals' identities. *Educational Management, Administration and Leadership, 34*(3), 297–337.

Blackmore, J., Thomson, P., and Sachs, J. (2005). *An investigation of the declining supply of school principals in two states in Australia*. ARC final report. Geelong: Deakin University.

Blase, J., and Blase, J. (2004). The dark side of school leadership: Implications for administrator preparation. *Leadership and Policy in Schools, 3*(4), 245–73.

Bloom, C. M., and Erlandson, D. (2003). African American women principals in urban schools: Realities, (re)constructions, and resolutions. *Educational Administration Quarterly, 39*(3), 339–69.

Blouin, P. (2005). *A profile of elementary and secondary school principals in Canada: First results from the 20045–2005 survey of principals*. Ottawa: Statistics Canada.

Boris-Schacter, S., and Langer, S. (2006). *Balanced leadership: How effective principals manage their work*. New York: Teachers College Press.

Bottery, M. (2000). *Education, policy and ethics*. London: Continuum.

Bowe, R., Ball, S., and Gold, A. (1992). *Reforming education and changing schools: case studies in policy sociology*. London: Routledge.

Breakwell, G. (2007). *The psychology of risk*. Cambridge: Cambridge University Press.

Breedon, K., Heigh, L., Leal, M., and Smith, L. O. (2001). *Principal power: Recruiting, retaining and rewarding quality principals*. Baltimore, MD: Shriver Centre.

Bridges, E. M. (1986). *The incompetent teacher: The challenge and the response*. Bristol: Falmer.

—— (1992). *The incompetent teacher: Managerial response*. London: Falmer.

Bright, T., and Ware, N. (2003). *Were you prepared? Findings from a national survey of headteachers*. Nottingham: NCSL.

Briner, R. B., Poppleton, S., Owens, S., and Kiefer, T. (2008). *The nature, causes and consequences of harm in emotionally-demanding occupations.* RR610. Norwich: Health and Safety Executive, UK.

Bristow, M., Ireson, G., and Coleman, A. (2007). *A life in the day of a headteacher: A study of practice and well being.* Nottingham: NCSL.

Britzman, D. (1994). Is there a problem with knowing thyself? Towards a poststructuralist view of teacher identity. In T. Shanahan (Ed.), *Teachers thinking, teachers knowing* (pp. 53–75). Urbana, IL: National Council of Teachers of English.

Brooking, K. (2004). Principals and school boards in New Zealand. Unpublished PhD thesis. Deakin University, Geelong, Australia.

Brown, K. M. (2004). Leadership for social justice and equity: Weaving a transformative framework and pedagogy. *Educational Administration Quarterly, 40*(1), 77–108.

Brundrett, M. (2001). The development of school leadership preparation programmes in England and the USA. *Educational Management and Administration, 29*(2), 229–45.

Burbules, N., and Torres, C. (Eds). (2000). *Globalisation and education: Critical perspectives.* London: Routledge.

Burchell, B. (2001). *Job insecurity and work intensification.* London: Routledge.

Bush, T., Glover, D., Sood, K., Cardno, C., Moloi, K., Potgeiter, G., *et al.* (2005). *Black and minority ethnic leaders.* Nottingham: NCSL.

Cain, J. (1999). The process of vision creation – intuition and accountability. In H. Tomlinson, H. Gunter and P. Smith (Eds), *Living headship: Voices, values and vision* (pp. 96–104). London: Paul Chapman.

Caldwell, B., and Spinks, J. (1988). *The self managing school.* London: Falmer Press.

—— (1992). *Leading the self managing school.* London: Falmer Press.

Case, P., Case, S., and Catling, P. (2000). Please show you're working: A critical assessment of the impact of OFSTED inspection on primary teachers. *British Journal of Sociology of Education, 21*(4), 605–21.

Casey, C. (1995). *Work, self and society: After industrialism.* London: Routledge.

Castles, F. (1991). *Australia compared: Politics and policies.* Sydney: Allen & Unwin.

Chaplain, R. P. (2001). Stress and job satisfaction among primary headteachers – a question of balance. *Educational Management and Administration, 29*(2), 197–215.

Chapman, C. (2002). Ofsted and school improvement: Teachers' perceptions of the inspection process in schools facing challenging circumstances. *School Leadership and Management, 22*(3), 257–72.

Chapman, J. (2005). *Recruitment, retention and development of school principals.* Brussels: International Academy of Education.

Chitty, C. (1997). Privatisation and marketisation. *Oxford Review of Education, 23*(1), 45–61.

Clandinin, D. J., and Connelly, F. M. (2000). *Narrative inquiry: Experience and story in qualitative research.* San Francisco: Jossey-Bass.

Clarke, L. (1999). *Mission improbable: Using fantasy documents to tame disaster.* Chicago: University of Chicago Press.

Codd, J. (2005). Teachers as 'managed professionals' in the global education industry: The New Zealand experience. *Educational Review, 57*(2), 193–206.

Coleman, A. (undated). *Collaborative leadership in extended schools: Leading in a multi-agency environment.* Nottingham: NCSL.

Coleman, M. (2005). *Gender and headship in the 21st century.* Nottingham: NCSL.

Conger, J. A., and Kanungo, R. N. (Eds). (1998). *Charismatic leadership in organisations.* Thousand Oaks, CA: Sage.

Cooley, V., and Shen, J. (2000). Factors influencing applying for urban principalship. *Education and Urban Society, 32*(4), 443–55.

Coser, L. A. (1974). *Greedy institutions: Patterns of undivided commitment.* New York: The Free Press.

Cosgrove, J. (2000). *Breakdown: The facts about stress in teaching.* London: RoutledgeFalmer.

Costrell, R., and Podursky, M. (2007). Peaks, cliffs and valleys: The peculiar incentives in teacher retirement systems and their consequences for school staffing. *ERIC.* ED 499007: Urban Institute.

Court, M. (1998). Women challenging managerialism: Devolution dilemmas in the establishment of co-principalships in primary schools in Aotearoa/New Zealand. *School Leadership and Management, 18*(1), 35–57.

—— (2003a). *Different approaches to sharing school leadership.* Nottingham: NCSL.

—— (2003b). Towards democratic leadership: Co-principal initiatives. *International Journal of Leadership in Education, 6*(2), 161–83.

—— (2004). Using narrative and discourse analysis in researching co-principalships. *International Journal of Qualitative Studies in Education, 17*(5), 579–603.

Craft, A., Jeffrey, B., and Leibling, M. (Eds). (2001). *Creativity in education.* London: Continuum.

Cranston, N. (2007). Through the eyes of potential aspirants: Another view of principalship. *School Leadership and Management, 27*(2), 109–28.

Cross, G. (1982). *The demon headmaster.* Oxford: Oxford University Press.

Crow, G. M. (undated). *School leader preparation: A short review of the knowledge base.*

Crow, G. M., and Matthews, L. J. (1998). *Finding one's way: How mentoring can lead to dynamic leadership.* Thousand Oaks, CA: Sage.

Cullingford, C. (Ed.). (1999). *An inspector calls: OfSTED and its effect on school standards.* London: Kogan Page.

Dahl, R. (1989). *Matilda.* London: Puffin Books.

Dale, R. (1999). Specifying global effects on national policy: A focus on the mechanisms. *Journal of Education Policy, 14*(1), 1–14.

Dantley, M. (2003). Purpose driven leadership: The spiritual imperative to guiding schools beyond high-stakes testing and minimum proficiency. *Urban Education, 35*(3), 273–91.

D'Arbon, T., Duignan, P., and Duncan, D. (2002). Planning for future leadership of schools: An Australian study. *Journal of Educational Administration, 40*(5), 468–85.

Daresh, J., and Male, T. (2000). Crossing the border into leadership: Experiences of newly appointed British headteachers and American principals. *Educational Management and Administration, 28*(1), 89–101.

Darling-Hammond, L., and Sykes, G. (2003). Wanted: A national teacher supply policy for education: The right way to meet the "highly qualified teacher" challenge. *Education Policy Analysis Archives, 11*(33).

Day, C. (2003). What successful leadership in schools looks like: implications for policy and practice. In B. Davies and J. West-Burnham (Eds), *Handbook of educational leadership and management* (pp. 187–204). London: Pearson, Longman.

Day, C., Harris, A., Hadfield, M., Tolley, H., and Beresford, J. (2000). *Leading schools in times of change.* Buckingham: Open University Press.

Dempster, N., and Berry, N. (2003). Blindfolded in a minefield: Principals' ethical decision-making. *Cambridge Journal of Education, 33*(3), 457–76.

Department for Education and Skills (DfES). (2007). *Gender and education: The evidence on pupils in England.* London: DfES.

Department for Education and Skills (DfES). (2007). *School workforce in England, January 2007*. London: National Statistics.

Donmoyer, R. (1999). The continuing quest for a knowledge base: 1976–98. In J. Murphy and K. S. Louis (Eds), *Handbook of research on educational administration: A Project of the American Educational Research Association* (pp. 25–44). San Francisco: Jossey-Bass.

Donmoyer, R., Imber, M., and Scheurich, J. (Eds.). (1995). *The knowledge base in educational administration: Multiple perspectives*. New York: State University of New York Press.

Dorman, J., and D'Arbon, T. (2003a). Assessing impediments to leadership succession in Australian Catholic schools. *School Leadership & Management, 23*(1), 25–40.

—— (2003b). Leadership succession in New South Wales Catholic schools: Identifying potential principals. *Educational Studies, 29*(2/3), 127–39.

Douglas, M. (1992). *Risk and blame: Essays in cultural theory*. London: Sage.

Draper, J., and McMichael, P. (1998). Preparing a profile: Likely applicants for primary school headship. *Educational Management and Administration, 26*(2), 161–72.

—— (2003). Keeping the show on the road? The role of the acting headteacher. *Educational Management and Administration, 31*(1), 67–81.

Dwyer, P., and Wynn, J. (2001). *Youth, education and risk: Facing the future*. London: RoutledgeFalmer.

Earley, P. (Ed.). (1998). *School improvement after inspection? School and LEA responses*. London: Paul Chapman Publishing.

Earley, P., Evans, J., Collarbone, P., Gold, A., and Halpin, D. (2002). *Establishing the current state of school leadership in England*. Research Report 336. London: DfES.

Eckman, E. W. (2006). Co-principals: Characteristics of dual leadership teams. *Leadership and Policy in Schools, 5*, 89–107.

Edmonds, E. L. (1968). *The first headship*. Oxford: Basil Blackwell.

Educational Research Service. (1998). *Is there a shortage of suitably qualified candidates for the principalship? An exploratory study*. Arlington, VA: National Association of Elementary School Principals and National Association of Secondary School Principals.

—— (2000). *Principal, keystone of a high achieving school: Attracting and keeping the leaders we need*. Arlington, VA: National Association of Secondary School Principals and National Association of Elementary School Principals.

Eilers, A. M., and Camacho, A. (2007). School culture change in the making: Leadership factors that matter. *Urban Education, 42*(6), 616–37.

Eirenreich, B. (2001). *Nickeled and dimed: On (not) getting by in America*. New York: Henry Holt.

—— (2005). *Bait and switch: The futile pursuit of the American dream*. New York: Henry Holt.

Eisinger, P. K., and Hula, R. C. (2004). Gunslinger school administrators: Nontraditional leadership in urban school systems in the United States. *Urban Education, 39*(6), 621–37.

Elmore, R. (2000). *Building a new structure for school leadership*. Washington, DC: Albert Shanker Institute.

Elsworth, J. (2007). *The paradox of being a principal: Supporter or assessor of underperforming teachers*. Canberra: Australian Primary Principals Association. Available on website: www.appa.edu.au. Accessed January 1, 2008.

English, F. (2000). Psst! What does one call a set of non-empirical beliefs required to be accepted on faith and enforced by authority?(Answer: a religion: aka the ISLLC standards). *International Journal of Leadership in Education, 3*(2), 159–67.

—— (2006). The unintended consequences of a standardized knowledge base in advancing educational leadership preparation. *Educational Administration Quarterly, 42*(3), 461–72.

—— (2008). *The art of educational leadership: Balancing performance and accountability*. Thousand Oaks, CA: Sage.

Estyn. (2007). *The impact of workforce remodelling on pupils' learning and raising standards*. Cardiff Estyn: Her Majesty's Inspectorate for Education and Training in Wales.

Evans, A. (2007). School leaders and their sensemaking about race and demographic change. *Educational Administration Quarterly, 43*(2), 159–88.

Evans, R. (1999). *The pedagogic principal*. Edmonton, Alberta: Qual Institute Press.

Fairclough, N. (2000). *New labour, new language*. London: Routledge.

Fidler, B., Earley, P., Ouston, J., and Davies, J. (1998). Teacher gradings and OfSTED inspection: Help or hindrance as a management tool? *School Leadership & Management, 18*(2), 257–70.

Fink, D. (1999). Deadwood didn't kill itself: A pathology of failing schools. *Educational Management and Administration, 27*(2), 131–41.

Forsyth, P., and Smith, T. (2002, April 1–5). Patterns of principal retention: What the Missouri case tells us. Paper presented at the American Education Research Association Annual Meeting, New Orleans.

French, S., and Daniels, G. (2007). *The NAHT work-life balance survey 2006*. London: National Association of Head Teachers. Available on http://www.naht.org.uk. Accessed April 23, 2007.

Frost, D., and Harris, A. (2003). Teacher leadership. *Cambridge Journal of Education, 33*, 479–98.

Fullan, M. (2006). *Turnaround leadership*. San Francisco: Jossey-Bass.

Gardner, H. (1996). *Leading minds: An anatomy of leadership*. New York: HarperCollins.

Garman, N. (1994). Qualitative inquiry: Meaning and menace for educational researchers. Paper presented at the Qualitative Approaches in Educational Research Seminar, Adelaide.

General Teaching Council for England (GTC). (2008). *Survey of teachers 2007: Teachers' careers and views on professional development*. London: GTC.

Gewirtz, S. (2002). *The managerial school: Post-welfarism and social justice in education*. London: Routledge.

Giddens, A. (1990). *The consequences of modernity*. Cambridge: Polity Press.

—— (1991). *Modernity and self identity*. Stanford, CA: Stanford University Press.

Gillbourn, D., and Youdell, D. (2000). *Rationing education: Policy, practice, reform and equity*. Buckingham: Open University Press.

Gilman, A., and Lanman-Givens, B. (2001). Where have all the principals gone? *Educational Leadership, 58*(8), 72–74.

Gilovich, T., Griffin, D., and Kahneman, D. (Eds). (2002). *Heuristics and biases: The psychology of intuitive judgment*. Cambridge: Cambridge University Press.

Gini, A. (2001). *My job, my self: Work and the creation of the modern individual*. New York: Routledge.

Gleeson, D., and Husbands, C. (Eds). (2001). *The performing school: Managing, teaching and learning in a performance culture*. London: RoutledgeFalmer.

Goodwin, F. J. (1968). *The art of the headmaster*. London: Ward Lock Educational.

Gorard, S., See, B. H., Smith, E., and White, P. (2007). What can we do to strengthen the teacher workforce? *International Journal of Lifelong Education, 26*(4), 419–37.

Green, F. (2001). It's been a hard day's night: The concentration and intensification of work in late twentieth century Britain. *British Journal of Industrial Relations, 39*(1), 53–80.

Gronn, P., and Lacey, K. (2004). Positioning oneself for leadership: Feelings of vulnerability among aspirant school principals. *School Leadership & Management, 24*(4), 405–24.

Gronn, P., and Lacey, K. (2006). Cloning their own: Aspirant principals and the school-based selection game. *Australian Journal of Education, 50*(2), 102–21.

Grubb, W. N., and Flessa, J. J. (2006). "A job too big for one": Multiple principals and other nontraditional approaches to school leadership. *Educational Administration Quarterly, 42*(4), 518–50.

Gunter, H. (1997). *Rethinking education: The consequences of Jurassic management.* London: Cassell.

—— (1999). Contracting headteachers as leaders: An analysis of the NPQH. *Cambridge Journal of Education, 29*(2), 251–64.

—— (2005). *Leading teachers.* London: Continuum.

Gunter, H., Rayner, S., Butt, G., Fielding, A., Lance, A., and Thomas, H. (2007). Transforming the school workforce: Perspectives on school reform in England. *Journal of Educational Change, 8*(1), 25–39.

Hall, C., and Noyes, A. (2008, March). Negotiating ethical teacher identities in performative school self evaluation systems. Paper presented at the American Educational Research Association Annual Meeting, New York.

—— (in press). The impact of school self evaluation processes of British teachers' views of their work and professionalism. *Research Papers in Education.*

Hallinger, P. (1992). The evolving role of American principals: From managerial to instruction to transformational leaders. *Journal of Educational Administration, 30*(3), 35–48.

Hallinger, P., and Bridges, E. M. (2007). *A problem based approach for management education: Preparing managers for action.* Dordrecht: Springer.

Handy, C. (1994). *The empty raincoat: Making sense of the future.* London: Hutchison.

—— (1995). *Beyond certainty: The changing worlds of organisations.* London: Hutchinson.

Hargreaves, A. (2003). *Teaching in the knowledge society: Education in the age of insecurity.* Buckingham: Open University Press.

—— (2004). Distinction and disgust: The emotional politics of school failure. *International Journal of Leadership in Education*, 27–43.

Hargreaves, A., and Fink, D. (2006). *Sustainable leadership.* San Francisco, CA: Jossey-Bass.

Harris, A. (2003). Teacher leadership as distributed leadership: Heresy, fantasy or possibility? *School Leadership and Management, 23*(3), 313–24.

—— (2008). *Distributed school leadership: Developing tomorrow's leaders.* London: Routledge.

Harris, A., and Chapman, C. (2002). *Effective leadership in schools facing challenging circumstances.* Nottingham: NCSL. Available http://www.ncsl.org.uk/research.

Harris, A., James, S., Gunraj, J., Clarke, P., and Harris, B. (2006). *Improving schools in exceptionally challenging circumstances: Tales from the frontline.* London: Continuum.

Harris, B. (2007). *Supporting the emotional work of school leaders.* London: Paul Chapman Publishing.

Hartley, F., and Thomas, K. (2005). *Growing tomorrow's school leaders: The challenge.* Nottingham: NCSL.

Harvey, D. (2005). *A brief history of neoliberalism.* Oxford: Oxford University Press.

Hatcher, R. (2005). The distribution of leadership and power in schools. *British Journal of Sociology of Education, 26*(2), 253–67.

Hayes, T. (2005). *Rising stars and sitting tenants: A picture of deputy headship in one London borough and how some of its schools are preparing their deputies for headship.* Nottingham: NCSL.

Heller, Z. (2003). *Notes on a scandal.* London: Viking.

Henry, J. (2006). *Creative management and development.* London: Sage.

Hochschild, A. R. (1997). *The time bind: When work becomes home and home becomes work.* New York: Metropolitan Books.

Holland, D., Lachicote, W., Skinner, D., and Cain, C. (1998). *Identity and agency in cultural worlds*. Cambridge, MA: Harvard University Press.

Hood, C. (1995). The "New Public Management" in the 1980s: Variations on a theme. *Accounting, Organisations and Society, 20*(2/3), 93 – 109.

—— (1998). *The art of the state: Culture, rhetoric and public management*. Oxford: Clarendon Press.

Hood, C., Rothstein, H., and Baldwin, R. (2001). *The government of risk: Understanding risk regulation regimes*. Oxford: Oxford University Press.

Hopkins, D., and Higham, R. (2007). System leadership: Mapping the landscape. *School Leadership and Management, 27*(2), 147–66.

Houle, J. (2006). Professional development for urban principals in underperforming schools. *Education and Urban Society, 38*(2), 142–59.

Howley, A., Andrianaivo, S., and Perry, J. (2005). The pain outweighs the gain: Why teachers don't want to become principals. *Teachers College Record, 107*(4), 757–82.

Howson, J. (2002). *17th survey of senior staff appointments in schools*. Wantage: Education Data Surveys.

—— (2008). *23rd annual report of senior staff appointments in schools in England and Wales*. Wantage: Education Data Surveys.

Hutter, B., and Power, M. (Eds). (2005). *Organisational encounters with risk*. Cambridge: Cambridge University Press.

Hyman, P. (2005). *1 out of 10: From Downing Street vision to classroom reality*. London: Vintage.

Irish Primary Principals Network (IPPN). (2004). *IPPN survey on principal's workload*. Dublin: IPPN.

Jansen, J. (2006). Leading against the grain: The politics and emotions of leading for social justice in South Africa. *Leadership and Policy in Schools, 5*, 37–51.

Jeffrey, B., and Woods, P. (1998). *Testing teachers: The effect of school inspections on primary teachers*. London: Falmer Press.

Johnson, B. (2003). Teacher collaboration: Good for some, not so good for others. *Educational Studies, 29*(4), 337–50.

Johnson, L. (2006). "Making her community a better place to live": Culturally responsive urban school leadership in historical context. *Leadership and Policy in Schools, 5*, 19–36.

Johnson, M. (1999). *Failing school, failing city*. Oxfordshire: Jon Carpenter Publishing.

Jones, K. (2003). *Education in Britain: 1944 to the present*. Oxford: Polity Press.

Jones, K., and Sinkinson, A. (2000). A critical analysis of OFSTED judgements of the quality of secondary Mathematics Initial Teacher Education courses. *Evaluation and Research in Education, 14*(2), 79–93.

Jordon, J., Gurr, E., Tinline, G., Giga, S., Faragher, B., and Cooper, C. (2003). *Beacons of excellence in stress prevention*. Research report 133. Norwich: Health and Safety Executive, UK Government.

Josselson, R., and Lieblich, A. (Eds). (1995). *Interpreting Experience: The narrative study of lives*. Thousand Oaks, CA: Sage.

Kamler, B., and Thomson, P. (2006). *Helping doctoral students write: Pedagogies for supervision*. London: Routledge.

Kaplan, I. (2008). Being 'seen', being 'heard': Engaging with students on the margins of education through participatory photography. In P. Thomson (Ed.), *Doing visual research with children and young people*. London: Routledge.

Karpinski, C. F. (2006). Bearing the burden of desegregation: Black principals and Brown. *Urban Education, 41*(3), 237–76.

Kenway, J., Bullen, E., Fahey, J., and Robb, S. (2006). *Haunting the knowledge economy*. New York: Peter Lang.

Kidd, J., Hirsh, W., and Jackson, C. (2004). Straight talk: the nature of effective career discussions at work. *Journal of Career Development, 30*(4), 231–45.

Kimball, K., and Sirotnik, K. (2000). The urban school principalship: Take this job and ... ! *Education and Urban Society, 32*(4), 535–43.

Kruger, M., Van Eck, E., and Vermeulen, A. (2001). Job mobility and premature departure of principals in primary and secondary education in the Netherlands. *School Leadership and Management, 21*(4), 397–413.

—— (2005). Why principals leave: Risk factors for premature departure in the Netherlands compared for women and men. *School Leadership & Management, 25*(3), 241–61.

Lacey, K. (2002). *Understanding principal class leadership aspirations: Policy and planning implications.* http://www.sofweb.vic.edu.au/pd/schlead/pdf/understanding_prin_class_leadership_aspirations_report.pdf. Accessed July 1, 2002. Melbourne, Victoria: Leadership Development Unit, Department of Education and Training.

Lacey, K., and Gronn, P. (2007). *Letting go: Former principals reflect on their role exit.* Melbourne: Centre for Strategic Education.

Lambert, L. (1998). *Building leadership capacity in schools.* Alexandria, VA: Association for Supervision and Curriculum Development.

Lambert, L., Walker, D., Zimmerman, D., Cooper, J., Lambert, M., Gardner, M., *et al.* (1995). *The constructivist leader.* New York: Teachers College Press.

Laming, D. (2004). *Human judgment: The eye of the beholder.* London: Thomson.

Lauder, H., Hughes, D., and Watson, S. (1999, April 19–23). The introduction of educational markets in New Zealand: questions and consequences. Paper presented at the American Educational Research Association Annual Meeting, Montreal.

Lawn, M., and Lingard, B. (2001). Constructing a European policy space in educational governance: The role of transnational policy actors. *European Educational Research Journal, 1* (2), 290–307.

Leithwood, K., and Day, C. (Eds). (2007). *Successful principalship. International perspectives.* Dordrecht: Springer.

Leithwood, K., Day, C., Sammons, P., Harris, A., and Hopkins, D. (2006). *Successful school leadership: What it is and how it influences pupil learning.* Research Report RR800. London: DfES.

Lieblich, A., Tuval-Masiach, R., and Zilber, T. (1998). *Narrative research: Reading, analysis and interpretation.* Thousand Oaks, CA: Sage.

Lipman, P. (1998). *Race, class, and power in school restructuring.* New York: State University of New York Press.

Loder, T. (2005). Women administrators negotiate work-family conflicts in changing times: An intergenerational perspective. *Educational Administration Quarterly, 41*(5), 741–76.

Loveless, A. (2002). *Literature review in creativity, new technologies and learning.* NESTA Futurelab.

Lumby, J. (2003). Distributed leadership in colleges: Leading or misleading? *Educational Management and Administration, 31*(3), 283–93.

Lupton, D. (Ed.). (1999). *Risk and sociocultural theory: New directions and perspectives.* Melbourne: Cambridge University Press.

Macbeath, J. (1999). *Schools must speak for themselves: The case for school self evaluation.* London: Routledge.

—— (2000). *Schools should speak for themselves.* London: Falmer.

—— (2006a). *School inspection and self-evaluation: Working with the new relationship.* London: Routledge.

—— (2006b). The talent enigma. *International Journal of Leadership in Education,* 9(3), 183–204.

Macbeath, J., Gray, J., Cullen, J., Frost, D., Steward, S., and Swaffield, S. (2007). *Schools on the edge: Responding to challenging circumstances.* London: Paul Chapman Publishing.

Macbeath, J., Jakobsen, L., Meuret, D., and Schratz, M. (2000). *Self evaluation in European schools: A story of change.* London: Routledge.

MacBeath, J., and Sugimine, H. (2002). *Self evaluation in the global classroom.* London: Routledge.

Macneil, W. K., and Topping, K. J. (2007). Crisis management in schools. Evidence based postvention. *Journal of Educational Enquiry,* 7(2), 1–20.

Maguire, M., Wooldridge, T., and Pratt-Adams, S. (2006). *The urban primary school.* Buckingham: Open University Press.

Mahony, P., and Hextall, I. (2000). *Reconstructing teaching: Standards, performance and accountability.* London: RoutledgeFalmer.

Male, T. (2001). Is the National Professional Qualification for Headship making a difference? *School Leadership and Management,* 21(4), 463–77.

Mander, M. (2008). *Critical incidents: effective responses and the factors behind them: An investigation into the factors that shape how leaders and teachers in school deal effectively with critical incidents and episodes.* Nottingham: NCSL.

Marginson, S. (1997). *Markets in education.* Sydney: Allen and Unwin.

Matthews, P., and Sammons, P. (2004). *Improvement through inspection: An evaluation of the impact of OfSTED's work.* London: OfSTED.

—— (2005). Survival of the weakest: the differential improvement of schools causing concern in England. *London Review of Education,* 3(2), 159–76.

McCormick, J. (1996). Occupational stress of teachers: Biographical differences in a large school system. *Journal of Educational Administration,* 35(1), 18–38.

McKenley, J., and Gordon, G. (2002). *Challenge plus: The experience of black and minority ethnic school leaders.* Nottingham: NCSL.

McLaughlin, T. (1996). *Street smarts and critical theory: Listening to the vernacular.* Madison, WI: University of Wisconsin Press.

McNamara, O., Howson, J., Gunter, H., Sprigada, A., and Onat-Selma, Z. (2008). *Women teachers' careers.* Birmingham: NASUWT.

McWilliam, E., and Singh, P. (2004). Safety in numbers? Teacher collegiality in the risk-conscious school. *Journal of Educational Enquiry,* 5(1), 22–33.

Menter, I., Hextall, I., and Mahony, P. (2003). Rhetoric or reality? Ethnic monitoring in threshold assessment of teachers in England and Wales. *Race, Ethnicity and Education,* 6(4), 307–29.

Mercer, D. (1997). The secondary headteacher and time-in-post: A study of job satisfaction. *Journal of Educational Administration,* 35(3), 268–81.

Militello, M., and Behnke, K. (2006, November 10–12). The principal shortage in Massachusetts: Discerning the need for credentialed candidates for qualified candidates. Paper presented at the Annual Meeting of the University Council for Educational Administrators, San Antonio, TX.

Ministerial Council of Employment Education Training and Youth Affairs (MCEETYA). (2003). *Demand and supply of primary and secondary school teachers in Australia.* http://www.mceetya.edu.au/public/demand.htm. Accessed September 1, 2003. Melbourne: MCEETYA.

Moller, J. (2006). Democratic schooling in Norway: Implications for leadership in practice. *Leadership and Policy in Schools,* 5, 53–69.

Moloi, K., and Potgieter, G. (2006). *Comparing the experiences of Black and Minority Ethnic leaders in English schools and cross-boundary leaders in South Africa.* Nottingham: NCSL.

Monroe, L. (1997). *Nothing's impossible: Leadership lessons from inside and outside the classroom.* New York: Public Affairs.

Moos, L., and Macbeath, J. (2004). *Democratic learning: The challenge to school effectiveness.* London: RoutledgeFalmer.

Mulford, B. (2003). *School leaders: Changing roles and impact on teacher and school effectiveness.* Paris: OECD.

Mullen, C., and Cairns, S. (2001). The principal's apprentice: Mentoring aspiring school administrators through relevant preparation. *Mentoring and Tutoring, 9*(2), 125–52.

Murphy, J. (2005). Unpacking the foundations of ISLLC Standards and addressing concerns in the academic community. *Educational Administration Quarterly, 41*(1), 154–91.

Murtadha, K., and Watts, D. M. (2005). Linking the struggle for education and social justice: Historical perspectives of African American leadership in schools. *Educational Administration Quarterly, 41*(4), 591–608.

Myers, K. (2005). *Teachers behaving badly? Dilemmas for school leaders.* London: RoutledgeFalmer.

Nader, K., and Pynoos, R. (1993). School disaster: Planning and initial intervention. *Journal of Social Behaviour and Personality, 8*(reprinted on http://www.giftfromwithin.org/html/nader.html. Accessed 27/9/2005).

National Association for Headteachers (NAHT). (2007). *The quick-reference handbook for school leaders.* London: Paul Chapman Publishing.

National College for School Leadership. (2007). *Greenhouse schools: Lessons from schools that grow their own leaders.* Nottingham: NCSL.

National Secondary Principals' Associations. (2007). *"Making a difference … Counting the cost". Research Report into School Leader Welfare.* www.aspa.edu.au Accessed April 23, 2008: Australian Secondary Principals Association, Australian Heads of Independent Schools, Catholic Secondary Principals Australia.

National Staff Development Council. (undated). *Learning to lead, leading to learn.* www.nsdc.org/library/leaders/leader-report.cfm: Accessed March 28, 2004.

Nippert-Eng, C. (1996). *Home and work: Negotiating boundaries through everyday life.* Chicago: University of Chicago Press.

O'Connor, M., Hales, E., Davies, J., and Tomlinson, S. (1999). *Hackney Downs: The school that dared to fight.* London: Cassell.

Office of Manpower Economics. (2000). *Teachers' workloads diary survey.* London: Office of Manpower Economics,

Owen, S., Kos, J., and McKenzie, P. (2008). *Staff in Australia's schools: Teacher workforce data and planning processes in Australia.* Canberra: Department of Education, Employment and Workplace Relations (DEEWR).

Partnership Project. (undated). *Governors supporting headteachers wellbeing.* Preston, Lancaster: The Wellbeing Team, Lancaster Local Authority.

Penn, H. (2002). "Maintains a good pace to lessons": Inconsistencies and contextual factors affecting OFSTED inspections of nursery schools. *British Educational Research Journal, 28*(6), 879 – 888.

Perry, L.-A. (2006). The impact of risk management on the changing nature of principal's work. Unpublished Ed D dissertation. Queensland University of Technology, Brisbane.

Perry, L.-A., and McWilliam, E. (2007). Accountability, responsibility and school leadership. *Journal of Educational Enquiry, 7*(1), 32–43.

Perryman, J. (2005). School leadership and management after Special Measures: Discipline without the gaze? *School Leadership & Management, 25*(3), 281–97.

Peters, M., Hitchings, M., Edwards, G., Minty, S., Seeds, K., and Smart, S. (2008). *Behavioural impact of changes in the Teachers' Pension Scheme.* Research Report RR024. London: DCSF.

Peters, T. (1992). *Liberation management.* New York: Alfred Knopf.

Pounder, D., Galvin, P., and Sheppard, P. (2003). An analysis of the United States educational administration shortage. *Australian Journal of Education, 47*(2), 133–45.

Pounder, D., and Merrill, R. (2001). Job desirability of the high school principalship: A job choice theory perspective. *Educational Administration Quarterly, 37*(1), 27–57.

Power, M. (2004). *The risk management of everything: Rethinking the politics of uncertainty.* London: Demos.

—— (2007). *Organised uncertainty. Designing a world of risk management.* Oxford: Oxford University Press.

Powney, J., Wilson, V., and Hall, S. (2003). *Teachers careers: The impact of age, disability, ethnicity, gender and sexual orientation.* London: DfES.

Preston, B. (2001). *Teacher supply and demand in states and territories.* Melbourne: Australian Council of Deans of Education.

—— (2002, December 1–5). Tracking trends in principal and teacher demand and supply. Paper presented at the Australian Association for Research in Education Annual Conference, University of Queensland, Brisbane.

PricewaterhouseCoopers. (2007). *Independent study into school leadership.* London: Department for Education and Skills. Available from http://www.dfes.gov.uk/research/ Accessed May 2, 2007.

Rassool, N., and Morley, L. (2000). School effectiveness and the displacement of equity discourses in education. *Race, Ethnicity and Education, 3*(3), 237–58.

Reay, D., and Ball, S. (2000). Essentials of female management: Women's ways of working in the education market place? *Educational Management and Administration, 28*(2), 145–59.

Rees, G., Power, S., and Taylor, C. (2007). The governance of educational inequalities: The limits of area-based initiatives. *International Journal of Comparative Policy Analysis, 9*(3), 261–74.

Reich, R. (1991). *The work of nations: A blueprint for the future.* New York: Simon and Schuster.

Rhodes, C., Brundrett, M., and Nevill, A. (2006). *The identification, development, succession and retention of leadership talent: An investigation within contextually different primary and secondary schools:* Manchester: The University of Manchester and The University of Birmingham.

Ribbins, P. (1999). Understanding leadership: Developing head teachers. In T. Bush, L. Bell, R. Bolam, R. Glatter and P. Ribbins (Eds), *Educational Management. Redefining theory, policy and practice* (pp. 77–89). London: Paul Chapman Publishing.

Rick, J., Briner, R. B., Daniels, K., Perryman, S., and Guppy, A. (2001). *A critical review of psychosocial hazard measures.* Norwich: Health and Safety Executive, UK Government.

Riessman, C. K. (1993). *Narrative analysis* (Vol. 30). Thousand Oaks, CA: Sage Publications.

Riley, D., and Mulford, B. (2006). England's National College for School Leadership: a model for leadership education? *Journal of Educational Administration, 45*(1), 80–98.

Riley, K., Hesketh, T., Rafferty, S., and Taylor-Moore, P. (2005). *Urban pioneers: Leading the way forward: First lesson from the Leadership on the Front-line project.* London: Institute of Education.

Robinson, J., and Godbey, G. (1997). *Time for life: The surprising way Americans use their time.* Pittsburgh, PA: Pennsylvania State Press.

Rosenthal, L. (2004). Do school inspections improve school quality? Ofsted inspections and school examination results in the UK. *Economics of Education Review, 23*, 143–51.

Roza, M., Celio, M. B., Harvey, J., and Wishon, S. (2003). *A matter of definition: Is there truly a shortage of school principals?* Washington, DC: Center on Reinventing Public Education, Daniel J. Evans School of Public Affairs, University of Washington.

Rusch, E. A. (2004). Gender and race in leadership preparation: A constrained discourse. *Educational Administration Quarterly, 40*(1), 14–46.

Samier, E. (2002). Weber on education and its administration: Prospects for leadership in a rationalised world. *Journal of Educational Management and Administration, 30*(1), 27–46.

Saulwick Muller Social Research. (2004). *The privilege and the price: A study of principal class workload and its impact on health and wellbeing.* Melbourne, Victoria: Department of Education and Training.

Sennett, R. (1998). *The corrosion of character: The personal consequences of work in the new capitalism.* New York: W.W. Norton & Company.

Sergiovanni, T. (1992). *Moral leadership: Getting to the heart of school improvement.* San Francisco: Jossey Bass.

Shaw, I., Newton, D. P., Aitkin, M., and Darnell, R. (2003). Do OfSTED inspections of secondary schools make a difference to GCSE results? *British Educational Research Journal, 29*(1), 63–75.

Sherman, A. (2000). Women managing/managing women: The marginalisation of female leadership in rural school settings. *Educational Management and Administration, 28*(2), 133–43.

Sieber, A. (undated). *No regrets? Starting secondary headship.* Nottingham: NCSL.

Silverman, D. (1993). *Interpreting qualitative data: Methods for analysing talk, text and interaction.* London: Sage.

Smith, A., Brice, C., Collins, A., Matthews, V., and McNamara, R. (2000). *The scale of occupational stress: A further analysis of the impact of demographic factors and type of job. Research report 311.* Norwich: Health and Safety Executive, UK Government.

Smithers, A., and Robinson, P. (2006). *School headship: Present and future.* Buckingham: Centre for Education and Employment Research.

Smulyan, L. (2000). *Balancing acts: Women principals at work.* New York: State University of New York Press.

Smyth, J., and Hattam, R. (2001). 'Voiced' research as a sociology for understanding 'dropping out' of school. *British Journal of Sociology of Education, 22*(3), 401–15.

Southworth, G. (1995). *Looking into primary headship: A research based interpretation.* London: The Falmer Press.

Spillane, J. (2006). *Distributed leadership.* San Francisco: Jossey-Bass.

Starr, K. (2001). The roar behind the silence: Women principals and their work. Unpublished doctoral thesis. University of South Australia, Adelaide.

Starratt, R. (2003). *Centering educational administration: Cultivating meaning, community, responsibility.* Mahwah, N J: Lawrence Erlbaum.

Stevens, J., Brown, J., Knibbs, S., and Smith, J. (2005). *Follow-up research into the state of school leadership in England.* Research Report RR633. Norwich: Department for Education and Skills.

Strike, K. (1994). Discourse ethics and restructuring. In *Philosophy of Education Yearbook,* http://www.ed.uiuc.edu/COE/EPS-Yearbook/94_docs/STRIKE.htm. Accessed 13 August 1998.

Strike, K., Haller, E., and Soltis, J. (1998). *The ethics of school administration* (2nd ed.). New York: Teachers College Press.

Stubbs, M. (2003). *Ahead of the class: How an inspiring headmistress gave children back their future.* London: John Murray.

Swaffield, S., and Macbeath, J. (2005). School self-evaluation and the role of a critical friend. *Cambridge Journal of Education, 35*(2), 239–52.

Tarleton, R. (2008). First person. *LDR, 30*(March), 27–28.

Taylor, S., Rivzi, F., Lingard, B., and Henry, M. (1997). *Educational policy and the politics of change*. London: Routledge.

Teacher Support Network. (2006). *The school well being report*. London: Teacher Support Network.

Thomson, P. (1994). *Local decision making and management*. Adelaide: Joint Principals Associations, South Australia.

—— (1997). *The changing role of the school principal*. CD-ROM. Adelaide, South Australia: South Australian Secondary Principals Association.

—— (1998). Thoroughly modern management and a cruel accounting: the effect of public sector reform on public education. In A. Reid (Ed.), *Going public: Education policy and public education in Australia* (pp. 37–46). Canberra: Australian Curriculum Studies Association.

—— (1999, May 8). Risky business: Principals and their learning in an age of insecurity. Paper presented at the Annual Principals Conference, Antigonish, Nova Scotia, Canada.

—— (2002). *Schooling the rustbelt kids: Making the difference in changing times*. Sydney: Allen & Unwin.

—— (2008a). Leading schools in high poverty neighbourhoods: The National College for School Leadership and beyond. In W. Pink and W. Noblit (Eds), *The international handbook of urban education* (pp. 1049–78). Dordrecht: Springer.

—— (2008b). Schools and urban regeneration: Challenges and possibilities. In B. Lingard, J. Nixon and S. Ranson (Eds) *Transforming learning in schools and communities*. London: Continuum.

Thomson, P., and Blackmore, J. (2006). Beyond the power of one: Redesigning the work of school principals and schools. *Journal of Educational Change, 7*(3), 161–77.

Thomson, P., Ellison, L., and Byrom, T. (2007). Invisible labour: home–school relations and the school front office. *Gender and Education, 19*(2), 141–58.

Thrupp, M. (1999). *Schools making a difference: Let's be realistic! School mix, school effectiveness and the social limits of reform*. Buckingham: Open University Press.

Tittle, D. (1995). *Welcome to Heights High: The crippling politics of restructuring America's public schools*. Columbus, OH: Ohio State University Press.

Tomlinson, S. (2001). *Education in post-welfare society*. Buckingham: Open University Press.

Tosey, P., and Nicholls, G. (1999). OfSTED and organisational learning: the incidental value of the dunce's cap as a strategy for school improvement. *Teacher Development, 3*(1), 5–17.

Toynbee, P. (2003). *Hard work: Life in low-pay Britain*. London: Bloomsbury.

Troman, G., and Woods, P. (2000). Careers under stress: Teacher adaptations at a time of intensive reform. *Journal of Educational Change, 1*(3), 253–75.

Wagner, J. (1993). Ignorance in educational research: Or, how can you not know that? *Educational Researcher, 22*(5), 15–23.

Warren Little, J. (2003). Constructions of teacher leadership in three periods of policy and reform activism. *School Leadership & Management, 23*(4), 401–19.

Watson, J. (2002). *The martyrs of Columbine: Faith and the politics of tragedy*. New York: Palgrave Macmillan.

Watts, J. (1976). Sharing it out: The role of the head in participatory government. In R. S. Peters (Ed.), *The role of the head* (pp. 127–36). London: Routledge & Kegan Paul.

Weber, M. (1947). *Essays in sociology* (H. H. Gerth and C. W. Mills, Trans.). London: Kegan Paul, Trench, Trubner and Co.

Wenger, E. (1998). *Communities of practice: Learning, meaning and identity*. Cambridge: Cambridge University Press.

Whitaker, K. S. (2003). Principal role changes and influence on principal recruitment and selection: An international perspective. *Journal of Educational Administration, 41*(1), 37–54.

Whitaker, P. (1983). *The primary head.* London: Heinemann Educational Books.

White, P., and Smith, E. (2005). What can PISA tell us about teacher shortage? *European Journal of Education, 40*(1), 93–112.

Whitty, G. (2002). *Making sense of education policy.* London: Paul Chapman Publishing.

Whitty, G., Power, S., and Halpin, D. (1998). *Devolution and choice in education: The school, the state and the market.* Buckingham: Open University Press.

Wilkens, E. R. (1995). Lives of a rural principal. In R. Thorpe (Ed.), *The first year as principal: Real world stories from America's principals* (pp. 54–9). Portsmouth, NH: Heinemann.

Wilkinson, R. (2005). *The impact of inequality: How to make sick societies healthier.* London: Routledge.

Winkley, D. (2002). *Handsworth revolution: The odyssey of a school.* London: Giles De La Mare.

Winter, R. (2002). Truth or fiction: problems of validity and authenticity in narratives of action research. *Educational Action Research, 10*(1), 143–52.

Wolcott, H. (1973). *The man in the principal's office: An ethnography.* Prospect Heights, IL: Waveland Press.

Woodfield, R. (2007). *What women want from work: Gender and occupational choice in the 21st century.* Basingstoke: Palgrave Macmillan.

Yeatman, A. (1990). *Bureaucrats, technocrats, femocrats: Essays on the contemporary Australian state.* Sydney: Allen and Unwin.

Yerkes, D. M., and Guaglianone, C. L. (1998). Where have all the high school administrators gone? *Thrust for Educational Leadership, 28*(2), 10–24.

Zellner, L., Jinkins, D., Gideon, B., Doughty, S., and McNamara, P. (2002, April 1–5). Saving the principal: the evolution of initiatives that made a difference in the recruitment and retention of school leadership. Paper presented at the American Education Research Association Annual Meeting, New Orleans.

Index